The Growing Years

A wealth of reproducible pictures, patterns, and activity ideas for early childhood

By
Sherrill B. Flora

Cover design by
Terri Moll

Inside illustrations by
Julie Anderson

Publisher
Instructional Fair • TS Denison
Grand Rapids, MI 49544

Permission to Reproduce

Instructional Fair • TS Denison grants the right to the individual purchaser to reproduce the student activity materials in this book for noncommercial individual or classroom use only. Reproduction for an entire school or school system is strictly prohibited. No part of this publication may be reproduced for storage in a retrieval system, or transmitted in any form or by any means, electronic, mechanical, recording, or otherwise, without the prior written permission of the publisher. For information regarding permission write to:

Instructional Fair • TS Denison, P.O. Box 1650, Grand Rapids, MI 49501.

Credits:
Author: Sherrill B. Flora
Cover & Inside Illustrations: Julie Anderson
Cover Art Production: Terri Moll
Project Director: Sherrill B. Flora
Editor: Sherrill B. Flora
Graphic Layout: Deborah Hanson McNiff

Standard Book Number: 0-7424-0141-3
The Growing Years
Copyright © 2001 by Instructional Fair Group
3195 Wilson Avenue NW
Grand Rapids, MI 49544

All Rights Reserved • Printed in the USA

Content by Themes

Ideas for Using Patterns	5–6
Colors	7–32
Shapes	33–58
Community Helpers	59–84
Transportation	85–96
Nursery Rhymes	97–112
Numbers	113–176
Weather	177–188
The Farm	189–206
Basic Concepts	207–224
Alphabet	225–304
Wild Animals	305–317
Pets	318–328
Birds, Bugs, and Other Creepy Crawlies	329–342
Eating Well	343–354
Months of the Year	355–367
Days of the Week	368–376
Seasonal and Holiday	377–424
All About Me	425–436
Puzzle Fun	437–448

Alphabetical Pattern Index

911	68
airplane	88, 214
alien	220
alligator	228
ambulance	96
American flag	412
ant	228
anteater	228
apples	8, 223, 226, 227, 384
autumn	378
Baa, Baa, Black Sheep	102
badges	66
balloons	23, 32, 116, 161, 229, 231
balls	9, 125, 152, 218, 231
bananas	24
barn	194, 222
bat	216
bears	16, 126
bed	210
bees	156, 335
beetle	337
bicycle	90
birds	127, 321, 330, 331, 332, 333, 334
birthday cake	390, 391
block	168
boats	87, 93, 134, 230, 379
book	77
boy	184, 354
breads and rice	350
bugs	122, 158, 337
bunnies	see rabbits
bus	95
bus driver	70
butterflies	128, 140, 149, 154
calendars	356–367
candle	234
candy	146
candy cane	399
cap	233, 234
cars	23, 86, 165, 232
caterpillar	234
cats	17, 118, 205, 217, 234, 258, 320, 386
caves	126, 216
chair	211
cherry tree	411
chicken	201, 222
chicks	136, 421
children	182, 183, 185, 206
chimpanzee	309
chipmunks	170
circle	34
clothing	186, 187, 188
clouds	179, 214
clown	161
Columbus Day	379
cornucopia	388
cow	195
crayons	159
crocodile	316
cupid	407
dairy products	346
diamond	40
doctors	81, 83
dogs	26, 123, 172, 235, 237, 319
doll	237
doll house	139
donut	237
ducks	114, 199, 236, 237
Easter eggs	422
egg	238, 240
eggplant	240
elephant	239, 240, 307
Eskimo	240
family tree	430
farmer	190
farmer's wife	191
Father's Day	424
feather	243
fire truck	62
firefighter	60
firefighter's hat	61
fireplace	398
fish	117, 151, 176, 242, 243, 296, 297, 322
flamingo	27
flowers	25, 31, 219, 419
fly	339
food pyramid	344
football	243
fox	20, 243
frames	72, 426, 431
Friday	374
frogs	12, 121, 145, 241, 340
fruits	348
garbage can	80
garbage truck	79
gate	246
geese	204, 245
gerbil	327
giraffe	311
girl	183, 246, 353
glue	159
goats	198, 244, 246
gorilla	246, 308
grapes	14
guinea pig	324
hamster	325
hat	26, 65, 133, 247, 249
hearts	404, 406
helicopter	91, 249
Hey Diddle Diddle	108
Hickory, Dickory, Dock	98

hippo 312	nose 267	slide 209
horse 196, 224, 249, 326	nurse 82, 84	snake 341
house 219, 248, 249, 428	octagon 41	snowflakes 180
Humpty Dumpty 104	octopus...270	snowperson 397
hyena 317	Old King Cole 107	space shuttle......................................92
I have a dream 403	Old Mother Hubbard 110	spider...338
ice cream 27, 251, 252	orange juice 25	square 35
igloo...252	ornaments 394	squirrel 381
inchworm 250, 252	ostrich 270	star 39
iron 252	otter 270	stars 39, 148, 152, 220
It's Raining 112	oval 38	stop sign 64
Jack and Jill.......................................109	owls 127, 268, 269 270, 304, 382	sun 10, 178, 282
Jack Be Nimble................................101	pails 152	Sunday 376
jack-in-the-box...141, 253, 254, 255	panda 273	sunflower.....................................281, 282
jacks 255	parrot 314	sweets and fats................................351
jar 255	peas 272, 273	table...285
jelly beans..255	pencils 159	teddy bear 16, 210, 231
jewels...166	penguin 273	teeth brushing 352
kangaroo 258	pig 21, 197, 271, 273	telephone 285, 429
key 257, 258	Pilgrim 389	television 285
kites 28, 138, 142, 256, 258, 417	place setting 345	Thursday..373
ladybugs...........................163, 173, 336	Pledge of Allegiance 413	tigers 147, 315
lamb 261	police car 69	toy box 433
lamp 260, 261	police officer 63	tractor 192
leaves...173, 380	police officer's hat 65	traffic light..67
leprechaun..416	present 395	train 89
librarian 76	pumpkin 13, 383	trees 24, 215, 223, 393, 411
lily pad...121	Pussy Cat, Pussy Cat 103	triangle 36
Lincoln, Abraham 408	quarters..276	Tuesday..371
lined paper..427	queen 274, 276	turkey..387
lion 259, 261, 306	quiet 276	turtle 143, 283, 284, 285, 323
lion and lamb 418	quill 275	umbrella.......................286, 287, 288
Little Bo Peep 99	quilt 276	unicorn 288
Little Jack Horner 105	rain 182	United States 288
lizard..342	rabbits..........18, 120, 167, 203, 209,	valentine 291, 405
lock...261	277, 278, 279, 328, 420	van 94
log home 410	rainbow.......................................22, 279, 415	vase 291
mail box 75	rectangle 37	vegetables 290, 291, 349
mail carrier...73	reindeer...396	violin 289, 291
mail truck 74	rhino 313	wagons 218, 224, 292
Martin Luther King Jr. 402	ring 279	Washington, George 409
Mary, Mary, Quite Contrary 100	rocket...221	watch...294
maze puzzles 438–448	rooster 202	watermelon 294
meat and cheese 347	rose 279	Wednesday.......................................372
mice 131, 132, 175, 217, 264	rulers 159	Wee Willie Winkie 106
milk 264	sanitation engineer 78	wind 181
mirror 432	Santa Claus 392	window 135, 293, 294
Monday 370	Saturday..375	winter...401
monkey 262, 264	scarecrow.............................193, 378, 385	wolf 294
moon 221, 263	school..212	wreath..400
Mother's Day.....................................423	school bus..71	x-ray...297
mountain 208	seahorse..282	xylophone......................................295, 297
mountain climber 208	seal 280, 282	yak 300
Mulberry Bush 369–376	shamrock 414	yard 300
Native American 389	sheep 200	yarn 299, 300
necklace..267	shelf 213	yo-yo 298, 300
nest 265, 267	shovel 152	zebra 301, 303, 310
newt 266, 267	Sing-a-Song of Six Pence 111	zipper...303

Ideas for Using the Patterns

BOOKS

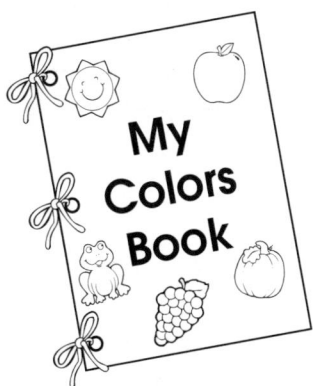

Individual "Take-Home" Books
The children will be able to make their own "take-home" books for each theme included in *The Growing Years*. Photocopy the pages that you would like to include in the children's individual books. Most themes will have a page that will look like the cover of the book (see illustration).

Punch holes along the side and secure with yarn or with brads.

You can add a "page-a-day" to the books or you may wish to give the children the books in complete form. How you chose to use individual books is up to the teacher.

Classroom Big Books
Choose your theme and enlarge each of the pages or patterns. Mount the patterns on 17 x 22-inch poster board. Small groups can work cooperatively on a page or you may wish to have individual children create a page for the "Classroom Big Book."

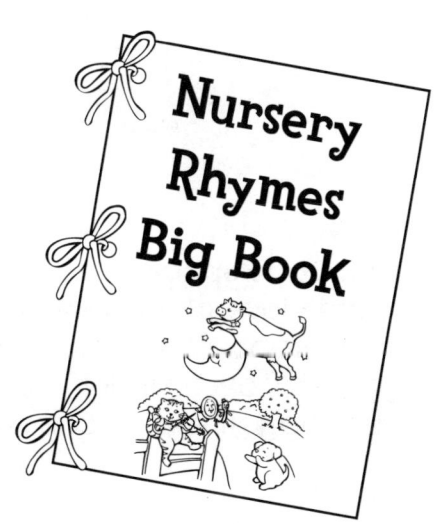

Punch holes along the side and secure with yarn, brads, or motal rings. The children will love to "read" their giant books that they have created for each theme that they are learning about!

FLANNEL BOARDS/MAGNETIC BOARDS

Flannel/Felt Boards
Photocopy the pattern, color, and cut-out. Laminate for durability. (If these are flannel board characters that the children are making to take home, you do not need to laminate them.)

Attach a small piece of self-stick Velcro on the back of each pattern piece. Self-stick Velcro adheres nicely to felt and flannel boards. You can also glue a small piece of sand paper to the back for use on a flannel board.

Magnetic Boards
Prepare the patterns the same way as you would the flannel board patterns. Purchase strips of magnetic tape (from hobby, hardware, or craft shops). Cut a small piece and attach to the back of each pattern. The magnetic strips will stick to magnetic boards, refrigerators, metal desk fronts, or metal classroom cabinets.

PUPPETS

Stick Puppets
Photocopy the pattern, color, and cut-out. Laminate for durability. (If these are puppets that the children are making to take home, you do not need to laminate them.) Using masking tape, tape a dowel rod, craft stick, tongue depressor, or paint stir stick to the back of the puppet. The children can sit on the floor behind a table or chair and use the stick puppets to make up their own stories or to retell a familiar story.

Marionette Puppets
Photocopy the pattern, color, and cut-out. Laminate for durability. (If these are puppets that the children are making to take home, you do not need to laminate them.) Tape a 2- to 3-foot piece of string on the back of the pattern (see illustration). Fold in half a 3 x 5-inch index card. Staple to the top of the string. Use the index card as a handle when manipulating the marionette.

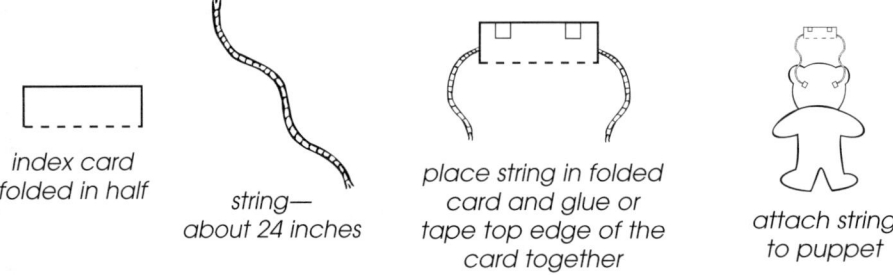

index card folded in half

string— about 24 inches

place string in folded card and glue or tape top edge of the card together

attach string to puppet

Paper Bag Puppets
Children love playing with paper bag puppets. They are the safest (no sticks) and the easiest puppets for young children to make "all-by-themselves." Photocopy the pattern, color, and cut-out. The children can glue the pattern onto the front of a lunch-size paper bag. The child can put his/her hand into the bag just like a hand-puppet.

BULLETIN BOARDS/MURALS

Cover the bulletin board (or wall) with white paper. Let the children draw and create the background scenery. You will want to guide the children according to the theme of the bulletin board. For a "Community Helpers" bulletin board, the children may wish to draw buildings for each of the "helpers." The children may wish to draw a large house for a bulletin board designed around the concept of "family." There are many possibilities with all the patterns in The Growing Years.

Photocopy the pattern, color, and cut-out. Once the background is complete, the children can tape or glue the completed patterns of people, animals, or objects.

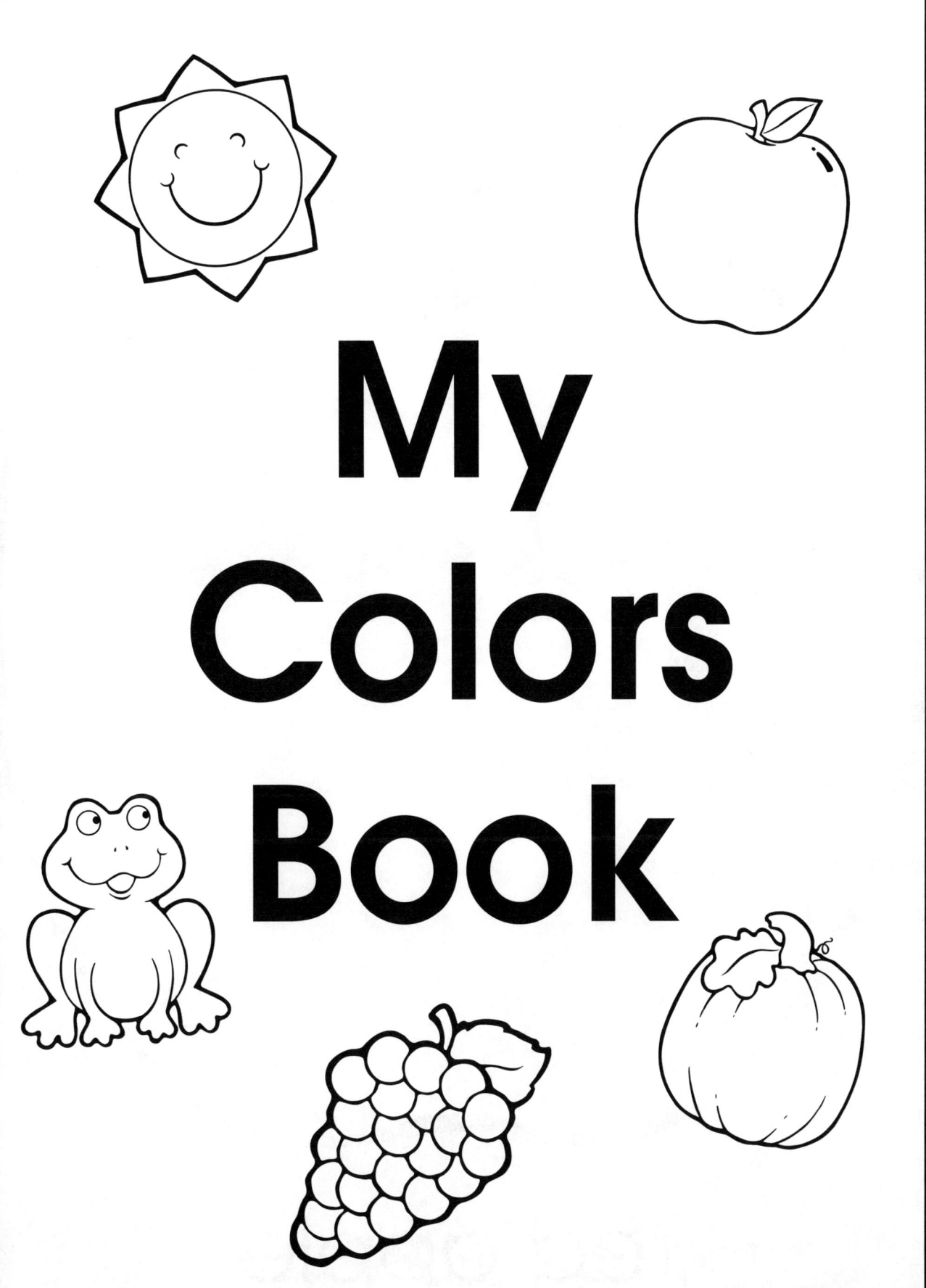

red apple

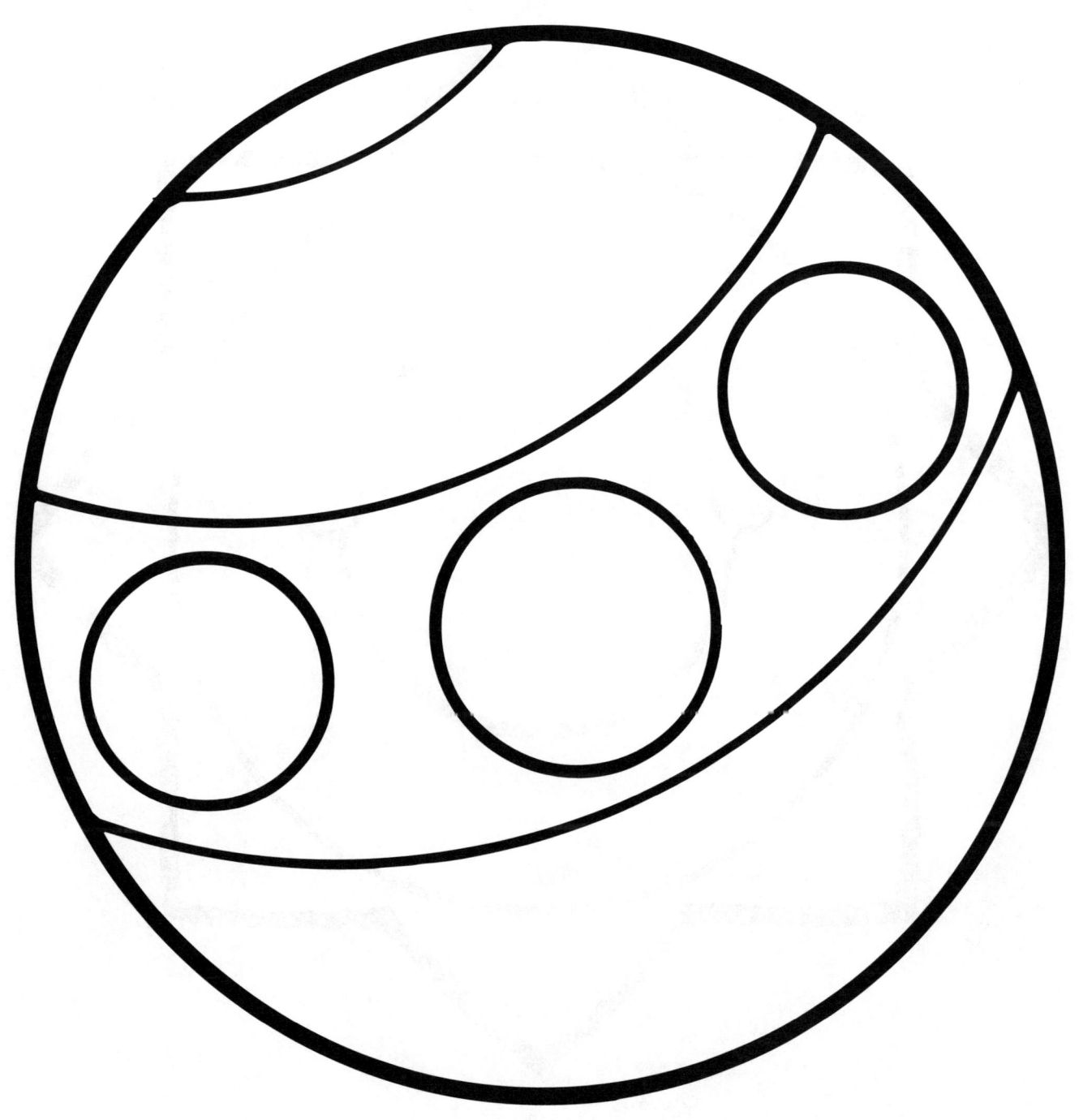

blue ball

yellow sun

Match

red

blue

yellow

green frog

orange pumpkin

purple grapes

Match

orange

green

purple

white bunny

Match

brown

white

black

gray fox

pink pig

Color the rainbow.

blue balloon

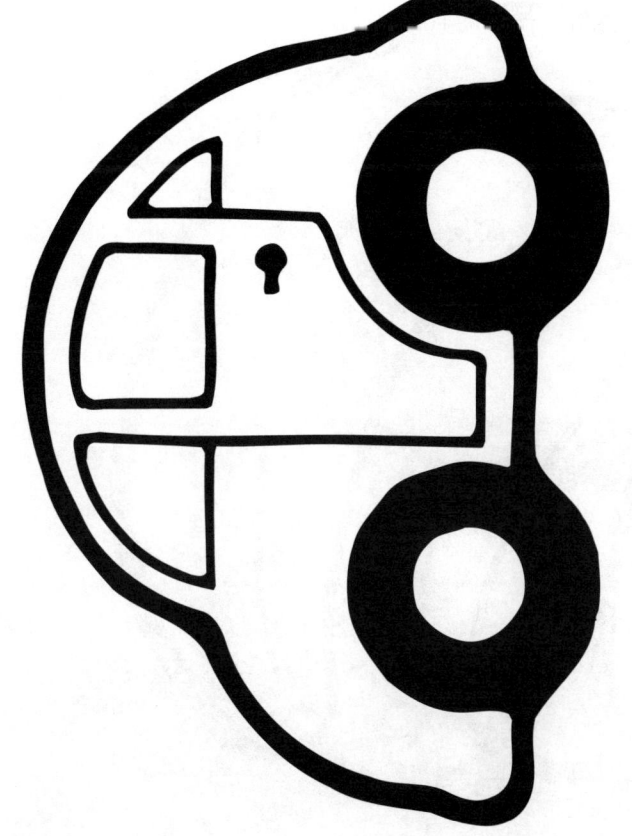

red car

green tree

yellow bananas

purple flowers

orange juice

black top hat

brown dog

pink flamingo

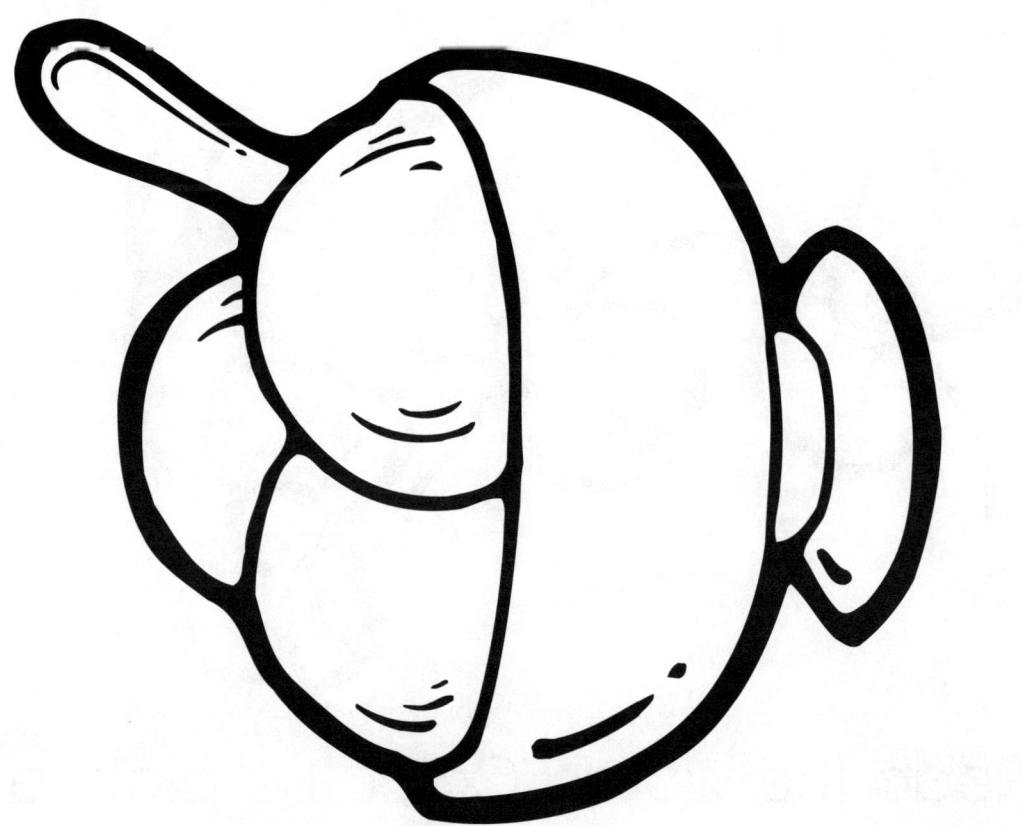

white ice cream

Read the words. Color the picture.

Read the words. Color the picture.

Read the words. Color the picture.

Read the words. Color the picture.

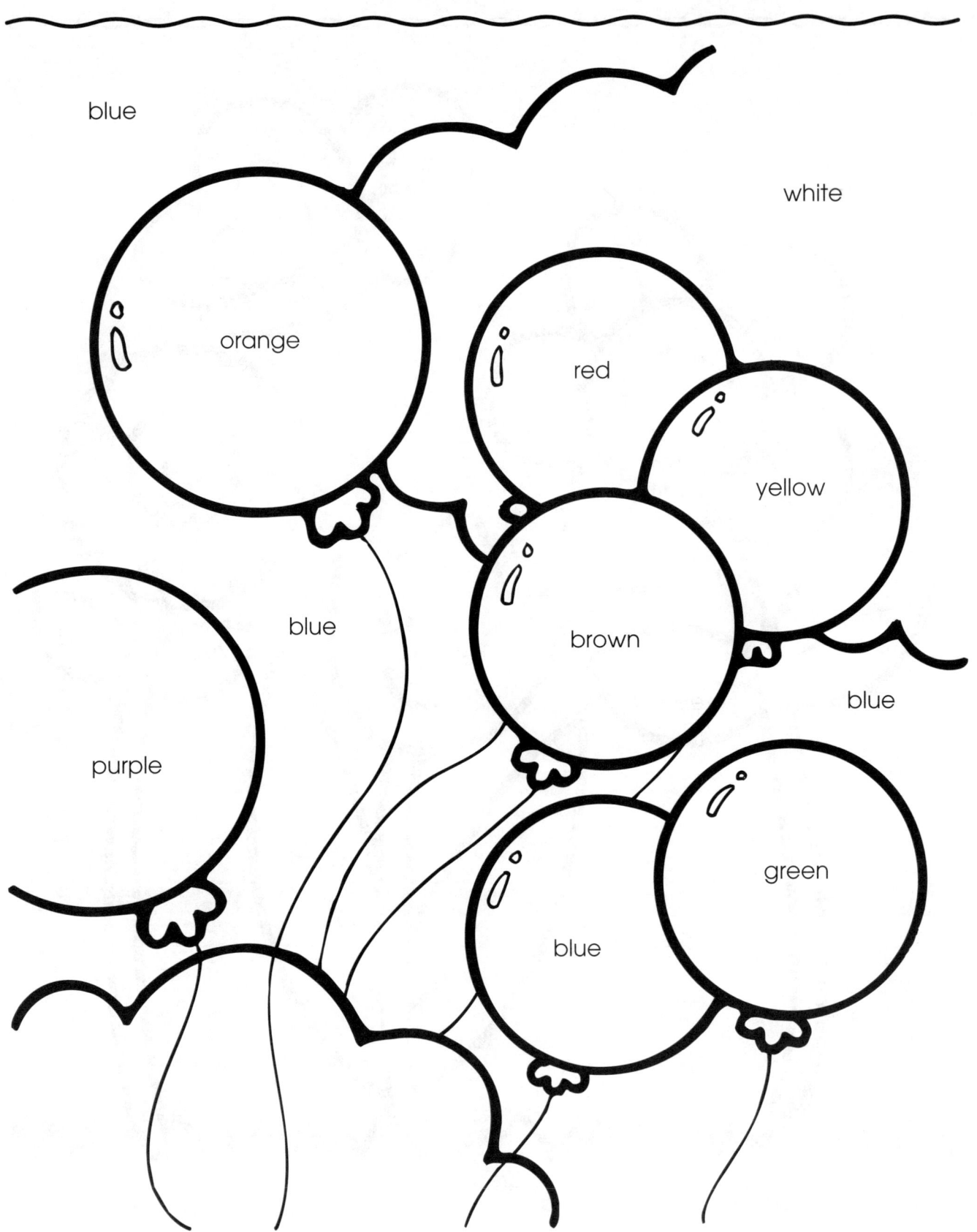

Read the words. Color the picture.

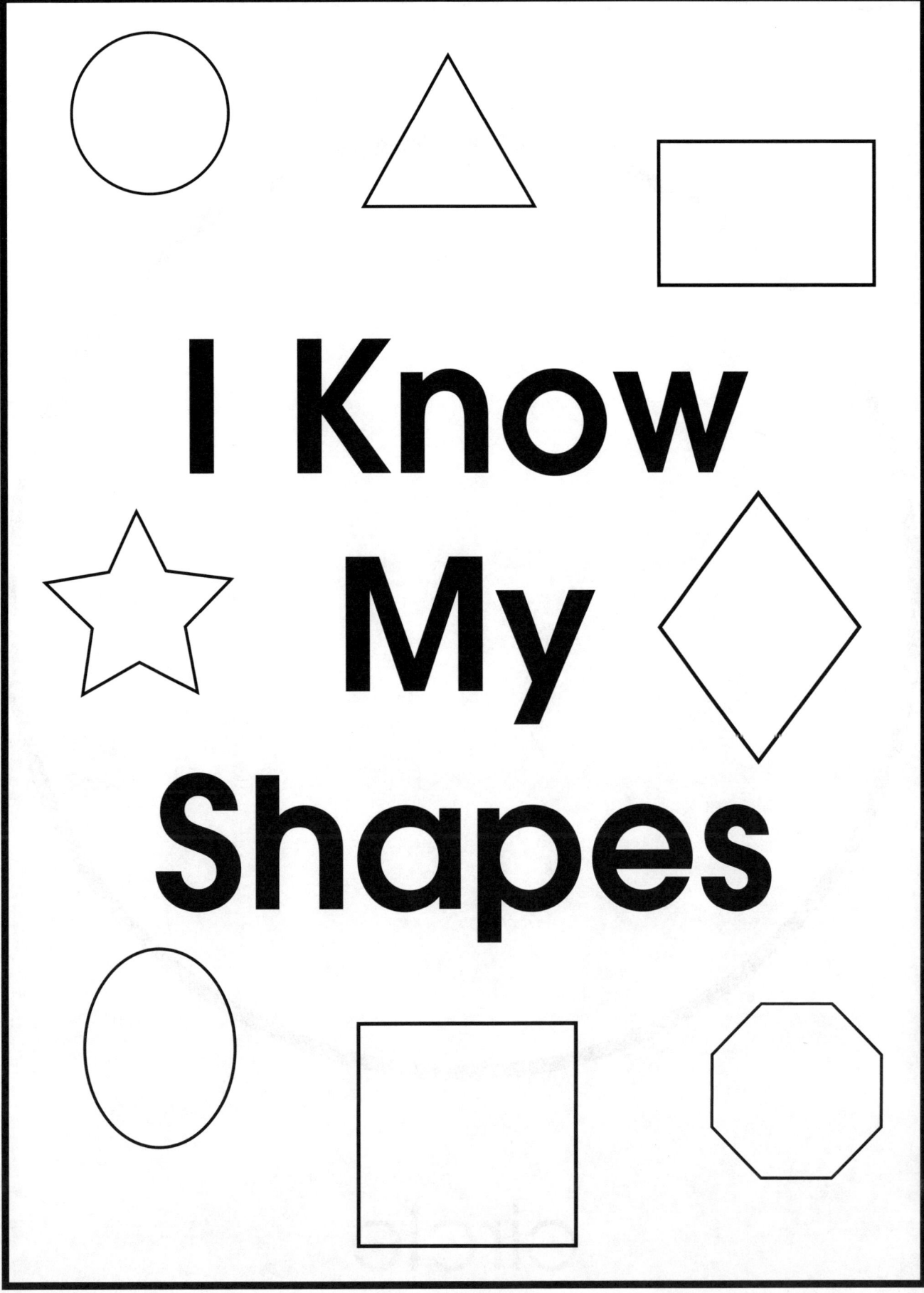

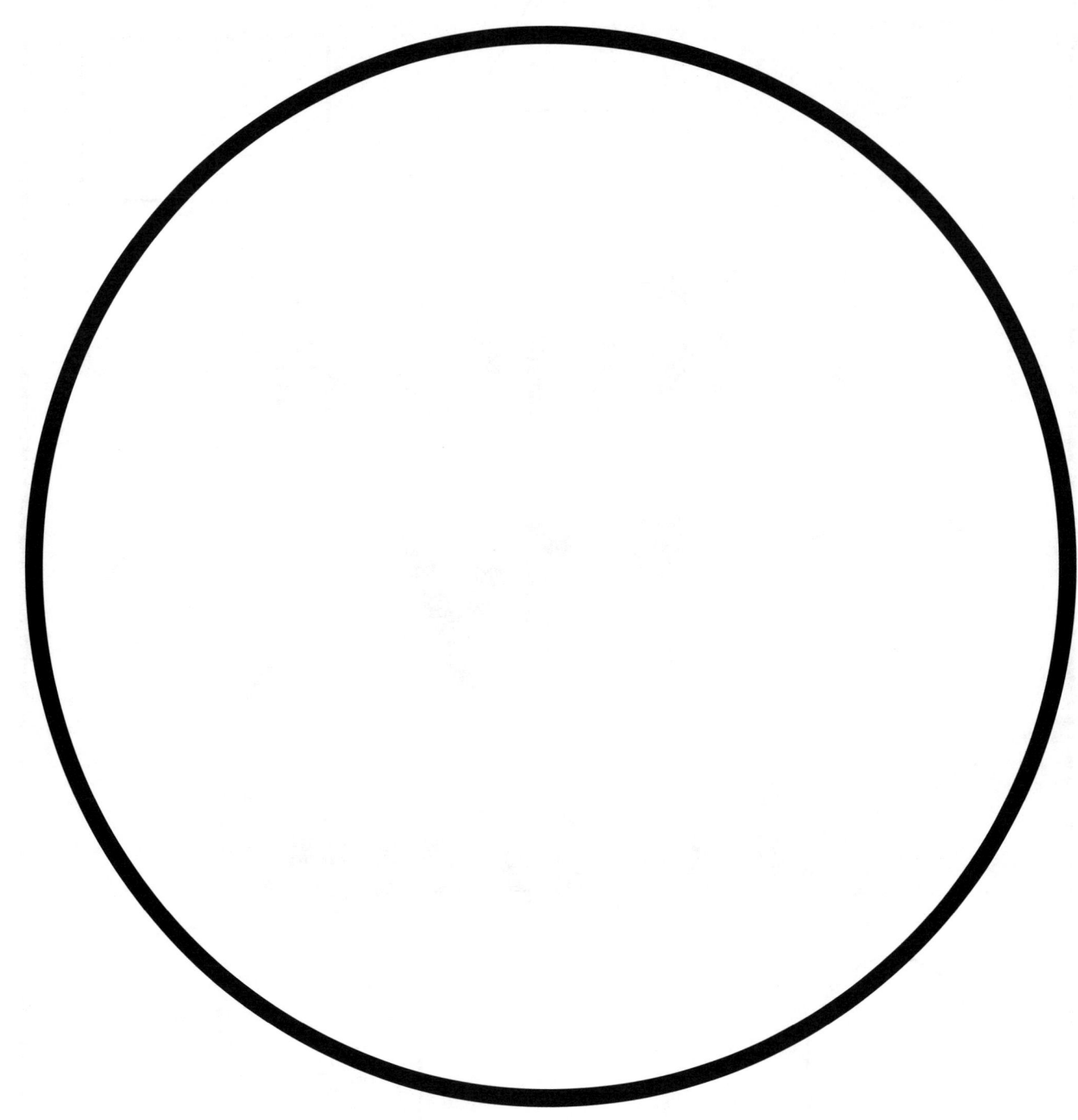

circle

square

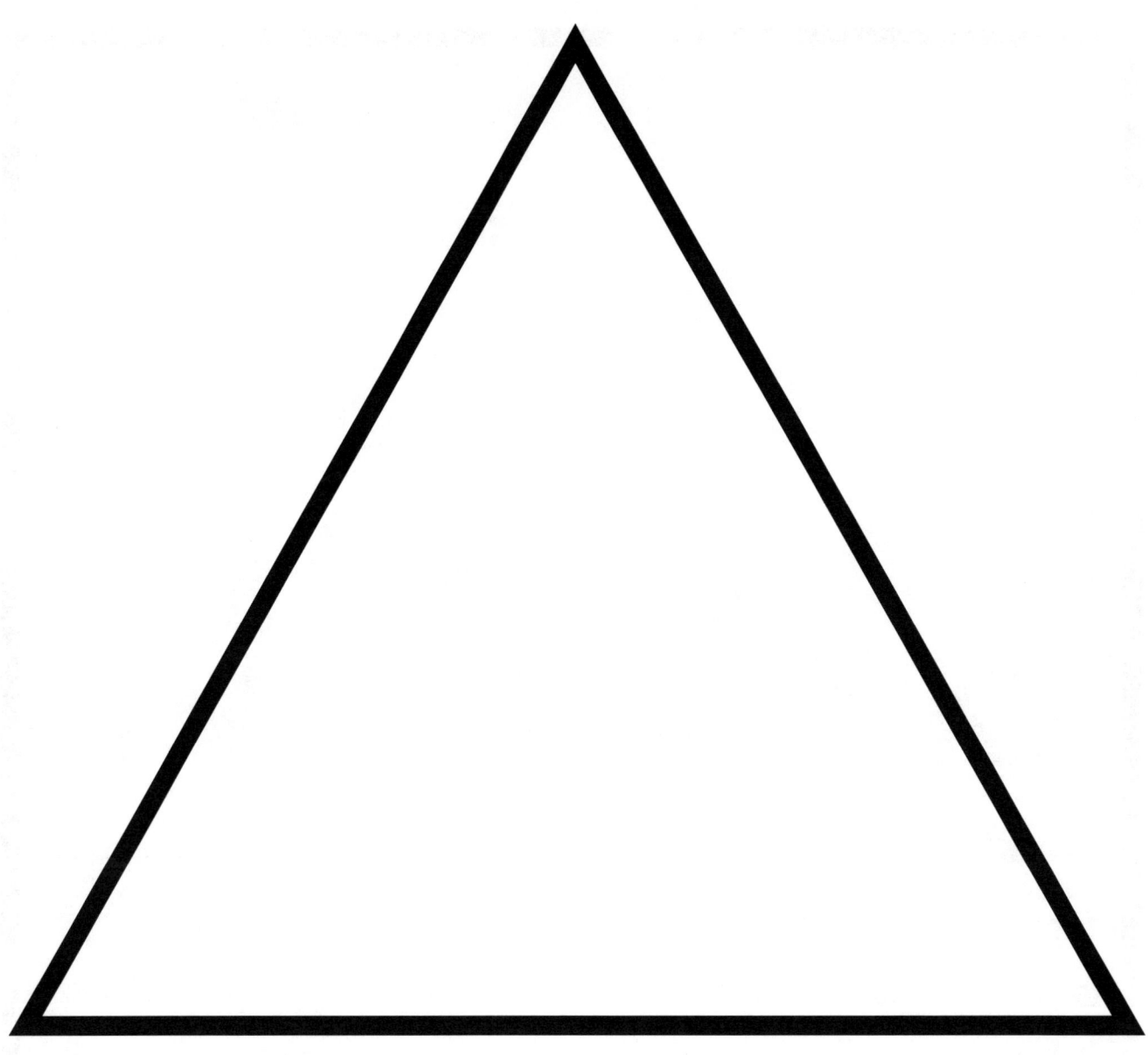

triangle

rectangle

oval

star

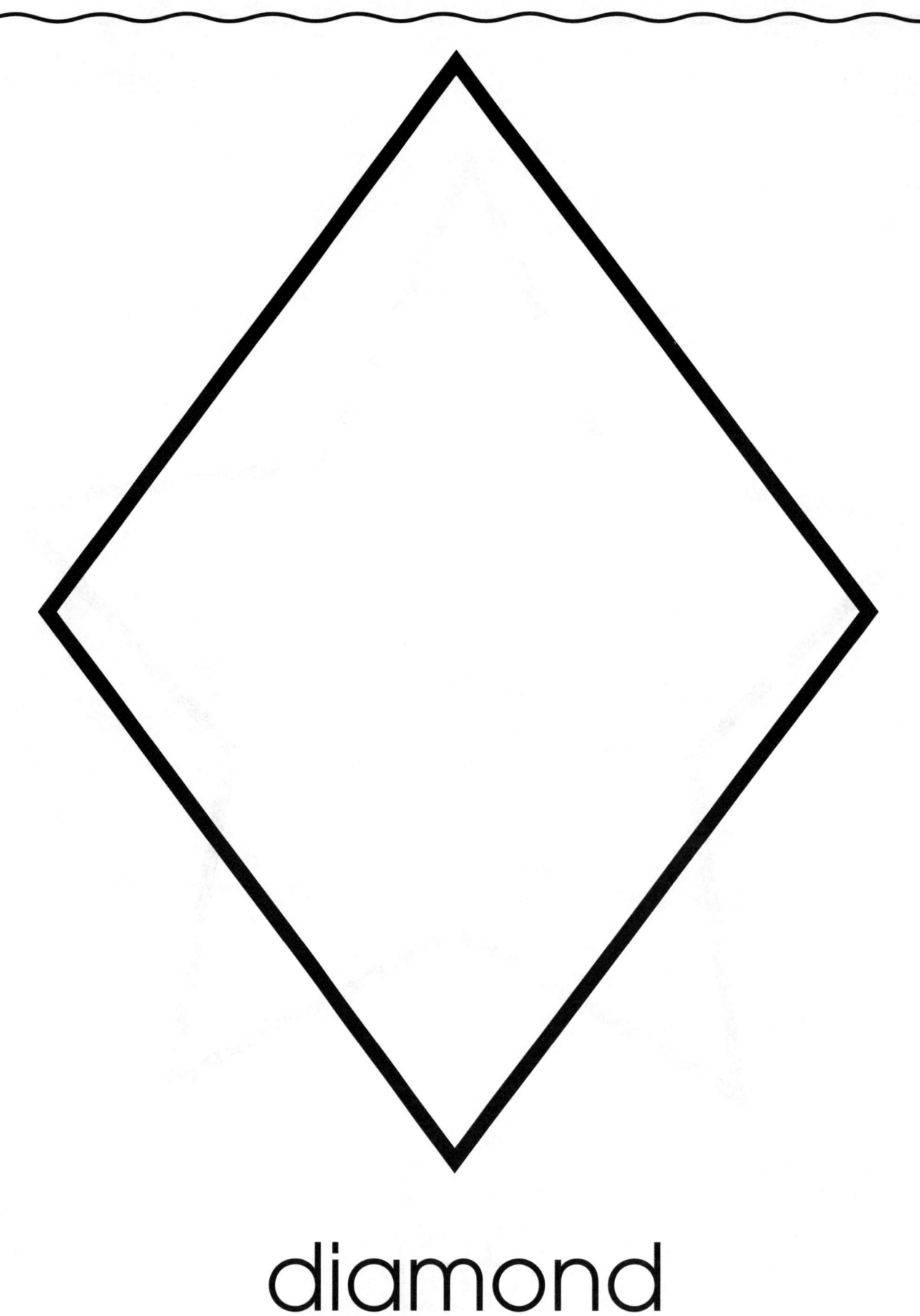

diamond

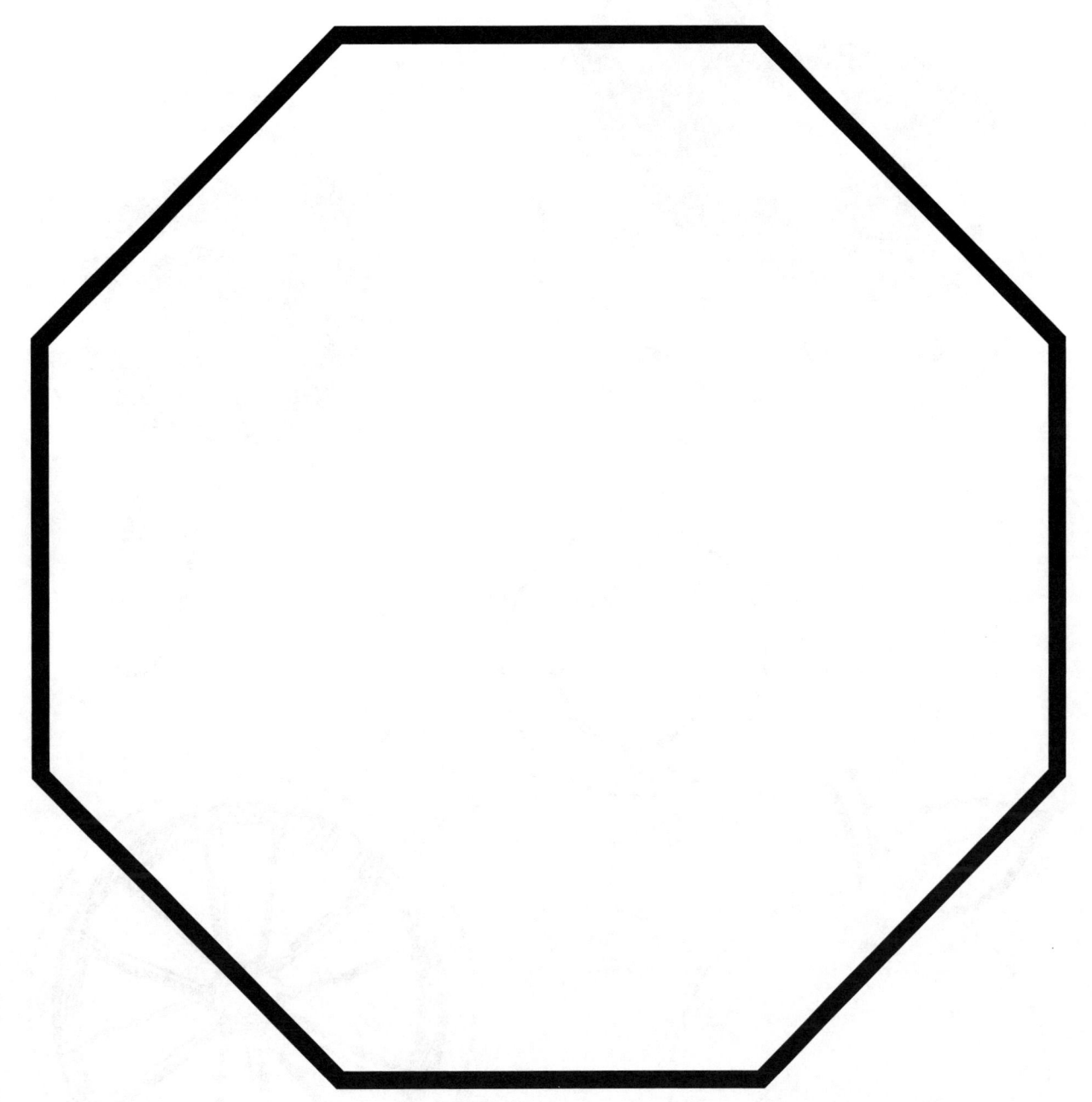

octagon

Trace all the circles.

Can you find all the circles?

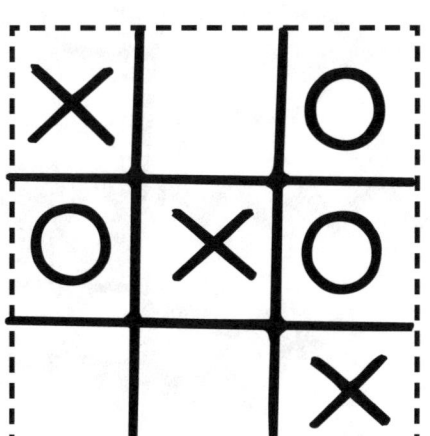

Trace all the squares.

Can you find all the squares?

Trace all the triangles.

Can you find all the triangles?

Trace all the rectangles.

Can you find all the rectangles?

Trace all the ovals.

Can you find all the ovals?

Trace all the stars.

Can you find all the stars?

Trace all the diamonds.

Can you find all the diamonds?

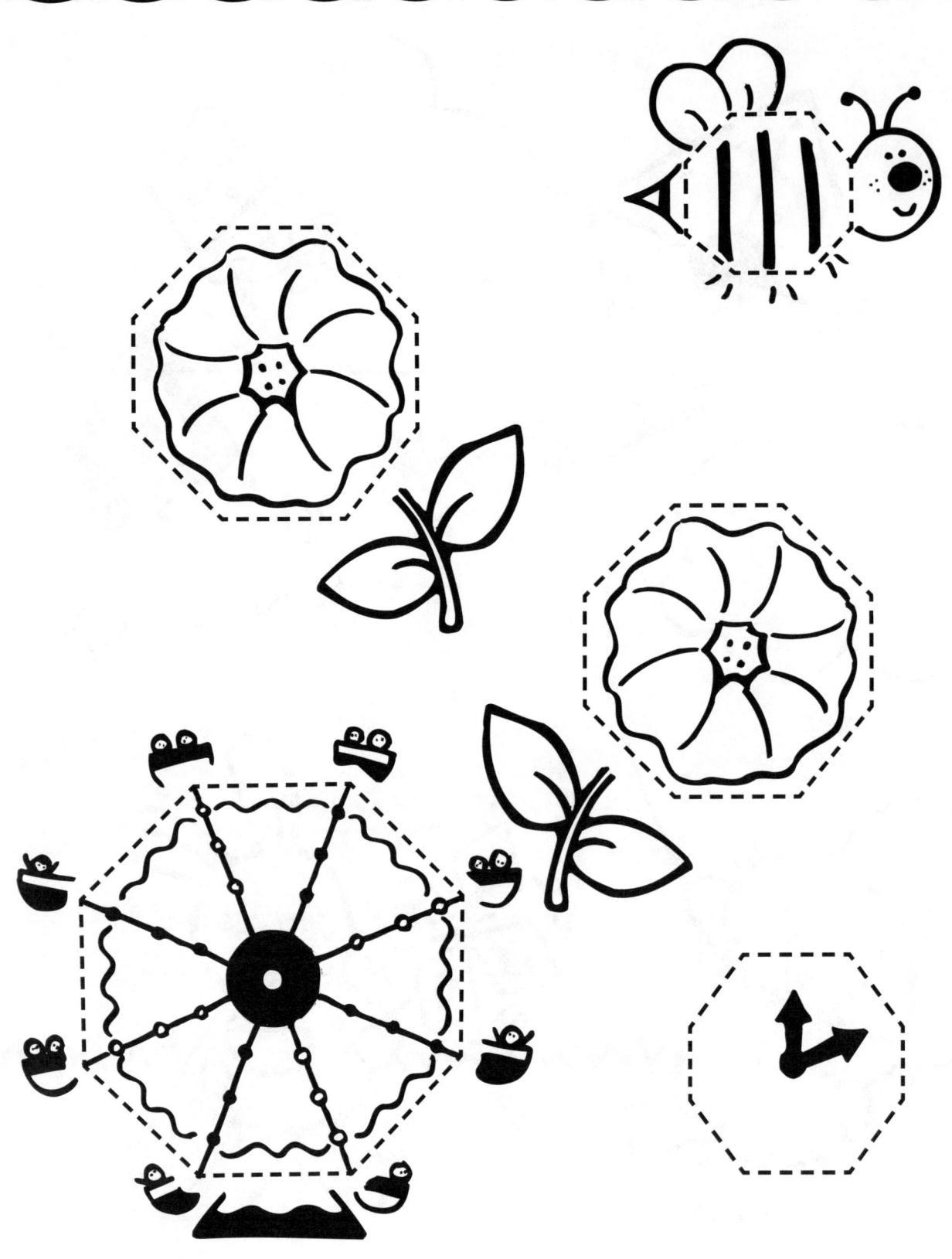

Trace all the octagons.

Can you find all the octagons?

Draw a line from the word to the shape.

circle

square

triangle

rectangle

diamond

octagon

star

oval

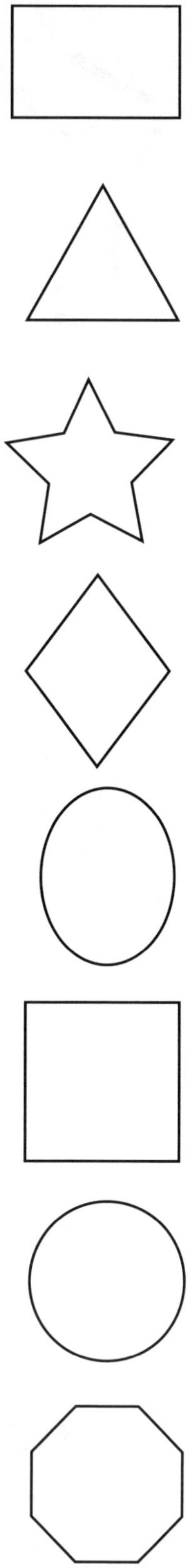

Community Helpers

This is a firefighter.

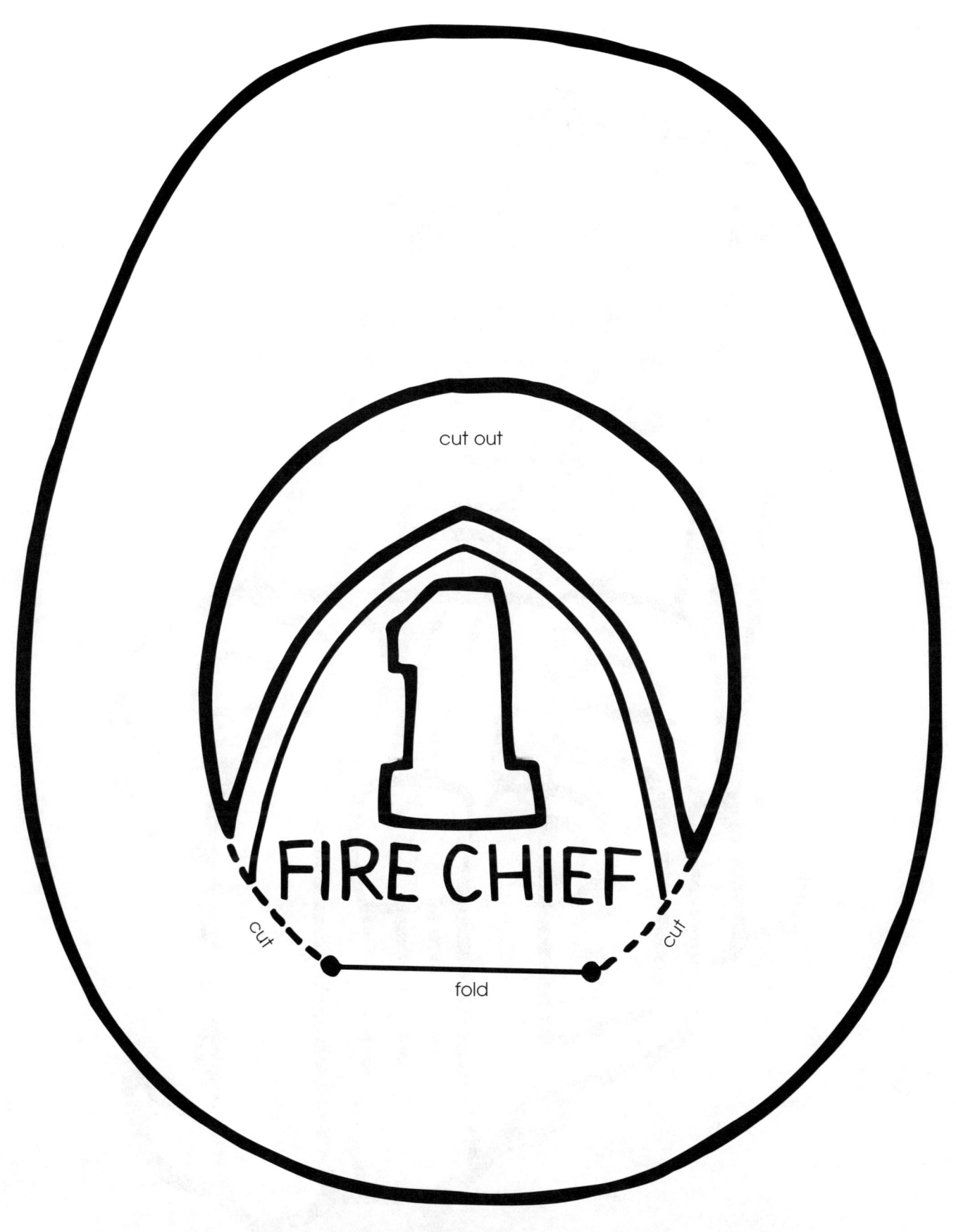

firefighter's hat

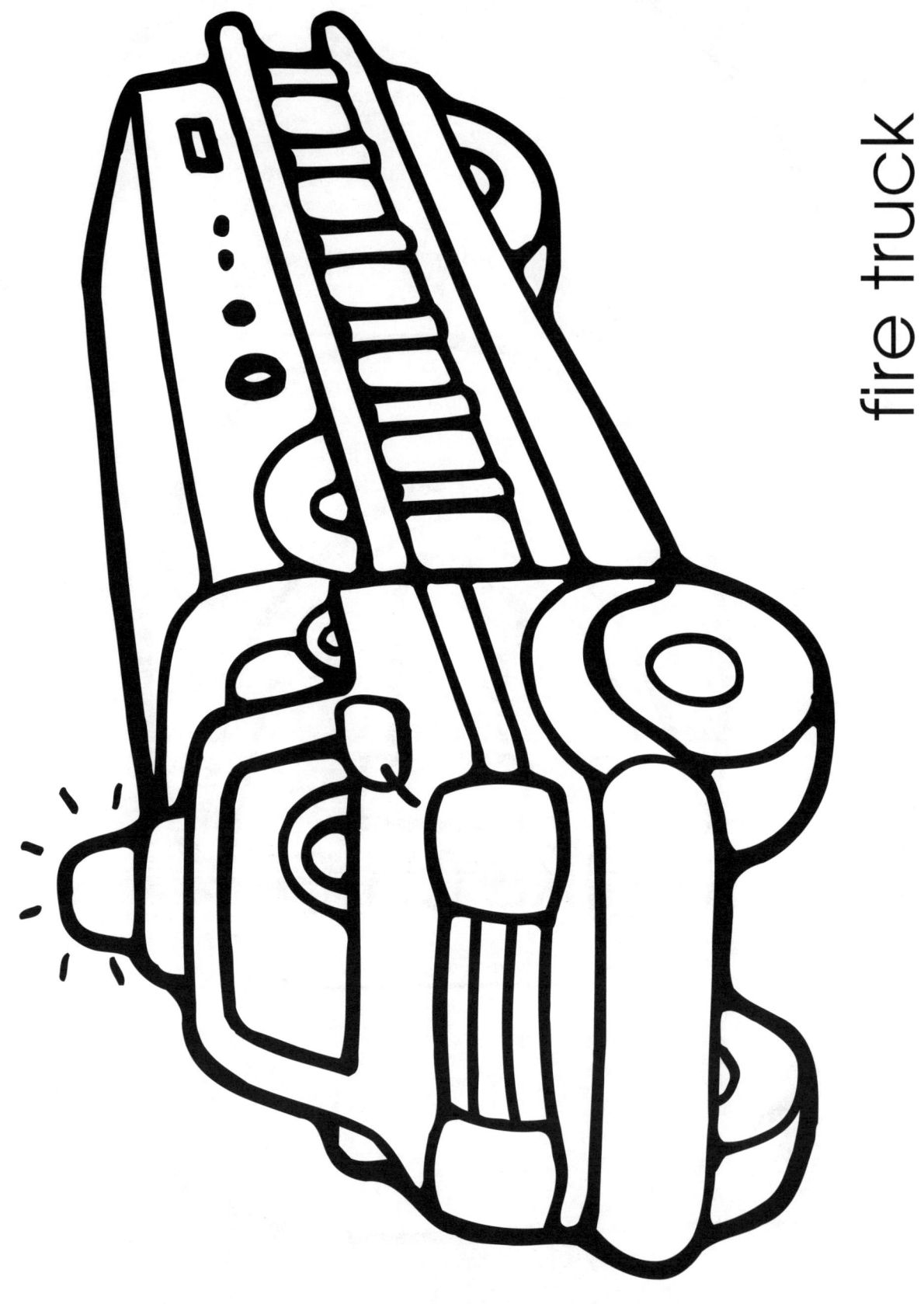

fire truck

This is a police officer.

stop sign

police officer's hat

Badges to color and decorate.

traffic light

Red on top means
stop, stop, stop!
Green below
means go, go, go!

police car

This is the bus driver.

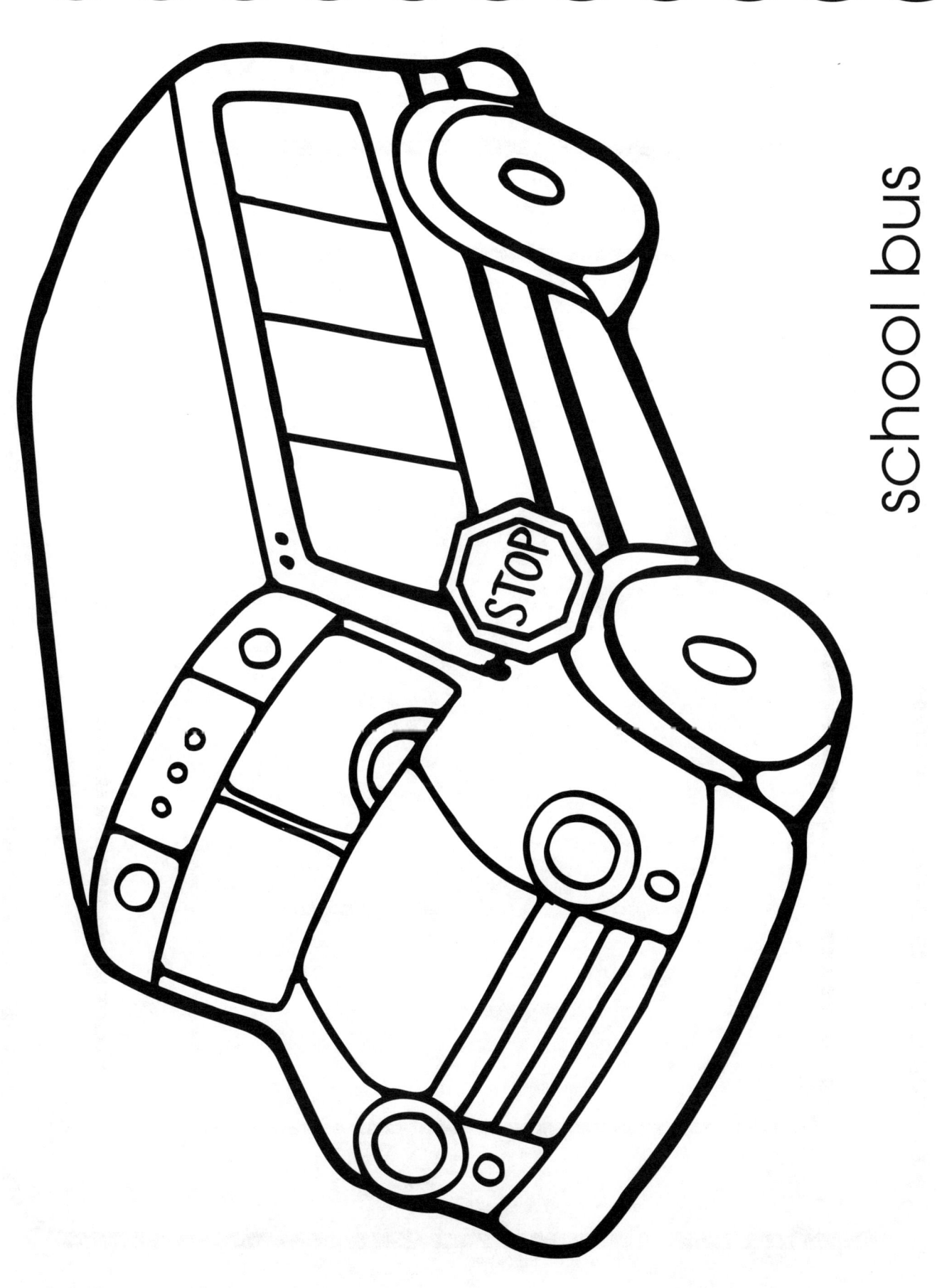

school bus

This is my teacher.

This is the mail carrier.

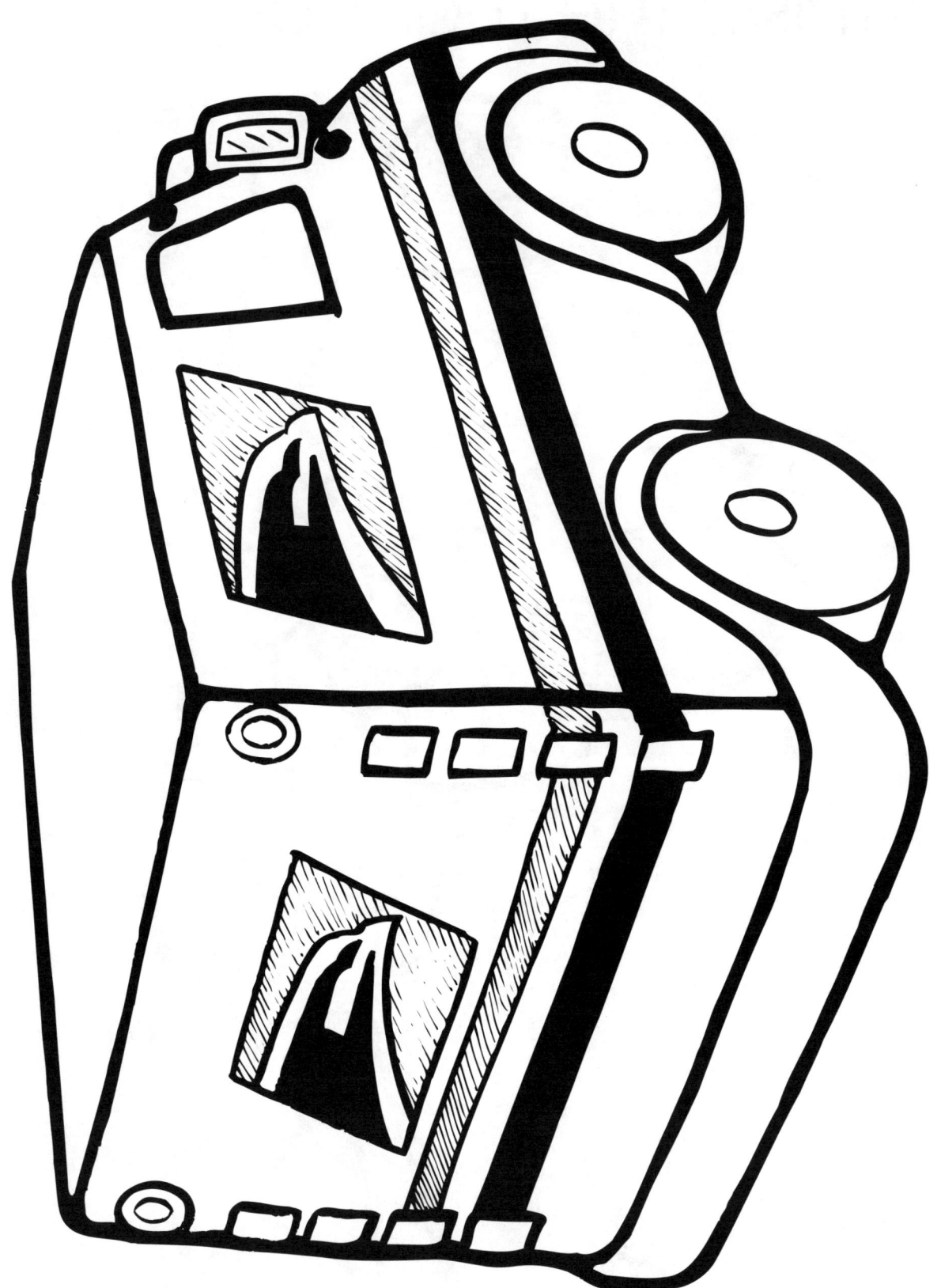

mail truck

mail box

This is the librarian.

We find books at the library.

This is the sanitation engineer.

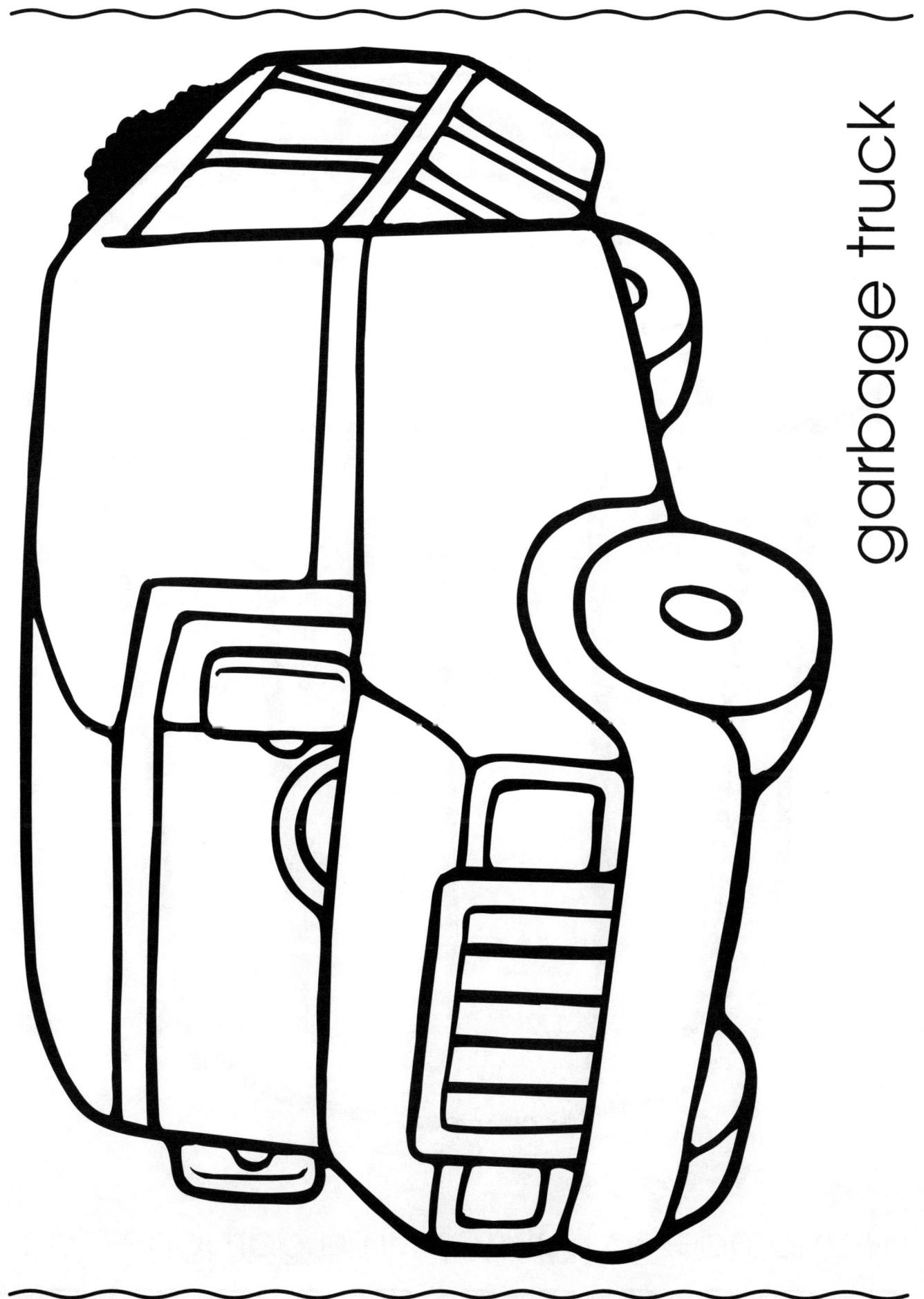

garbage truck

Remember to put trash in a garbage can.

This is the doctor.

This is the nurse.

This is the doctor.

This is the nurse.

Let's Learn About Transportation

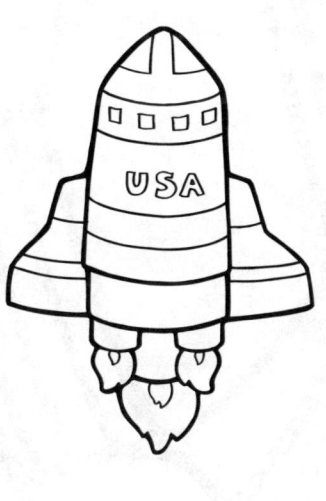

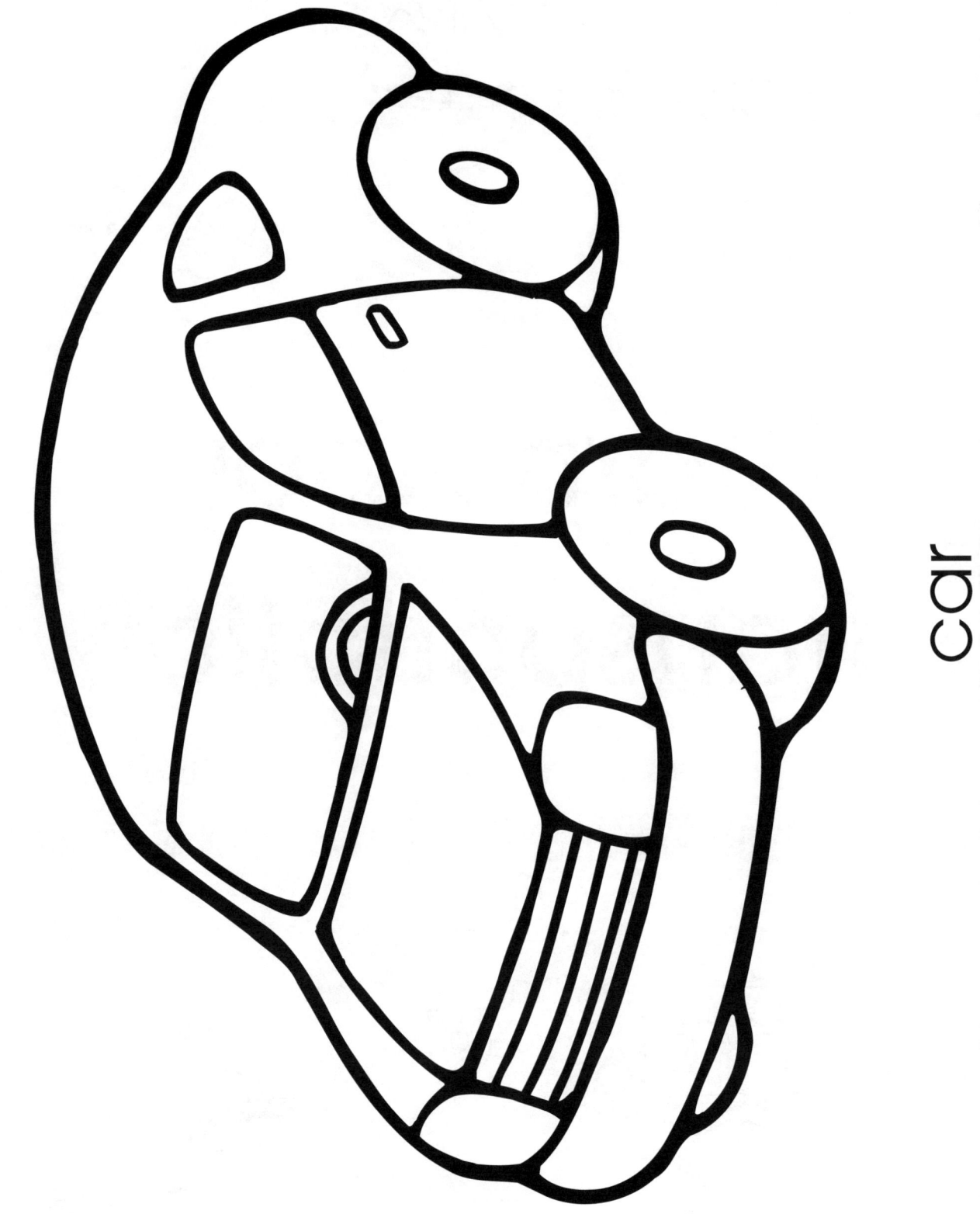
car

sailboat

airplane

train

bicycle

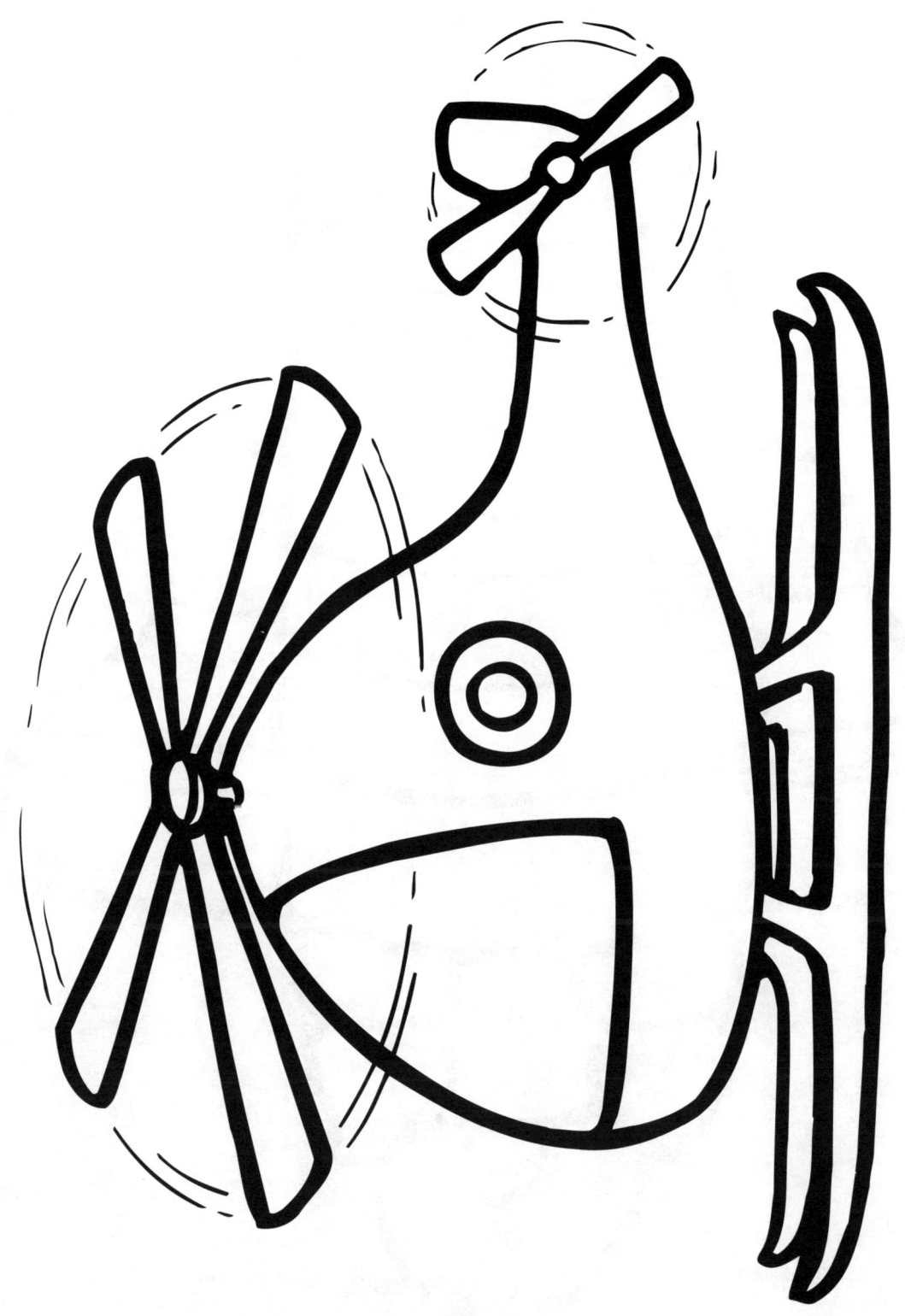

helicopter

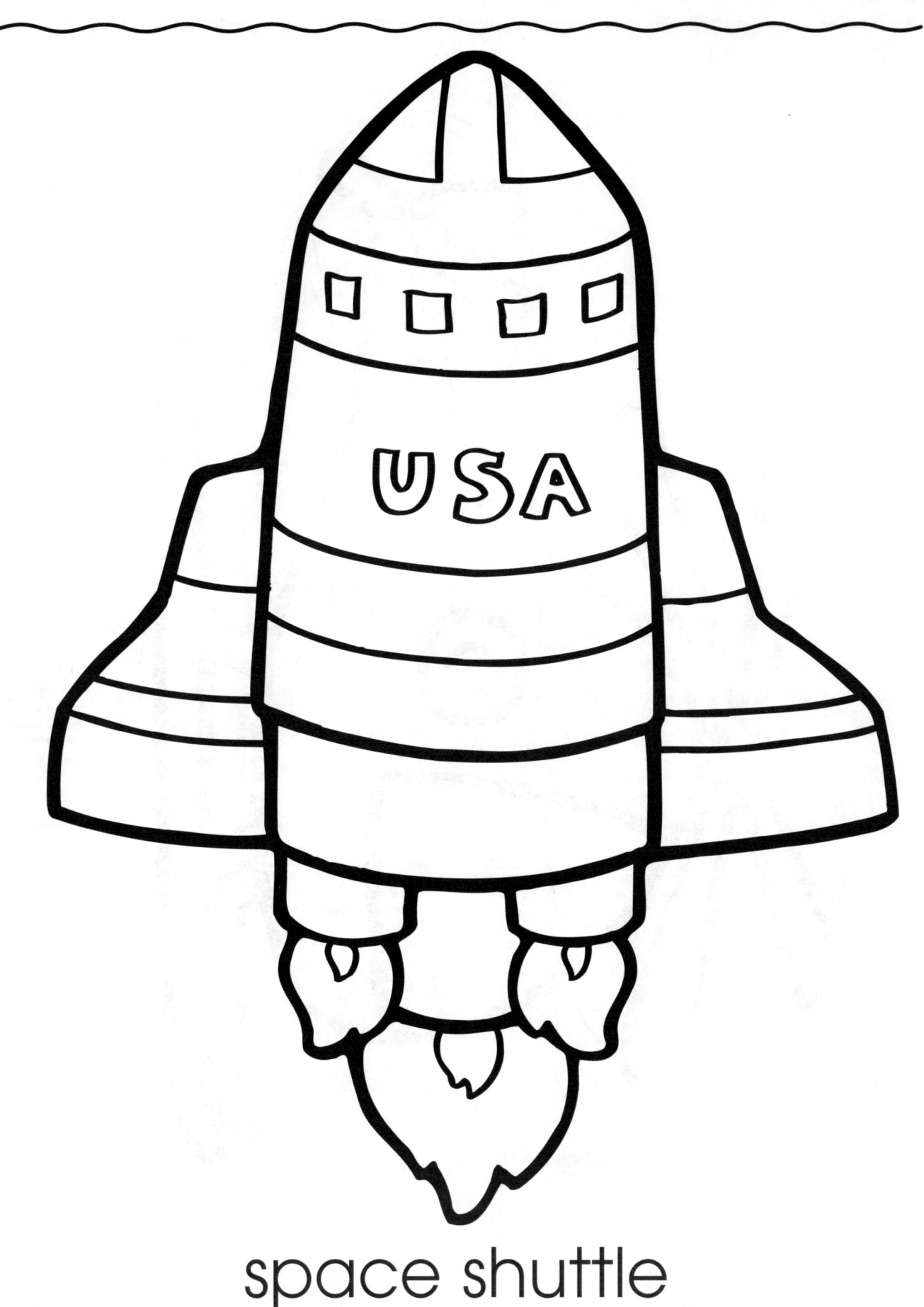

space shuttle

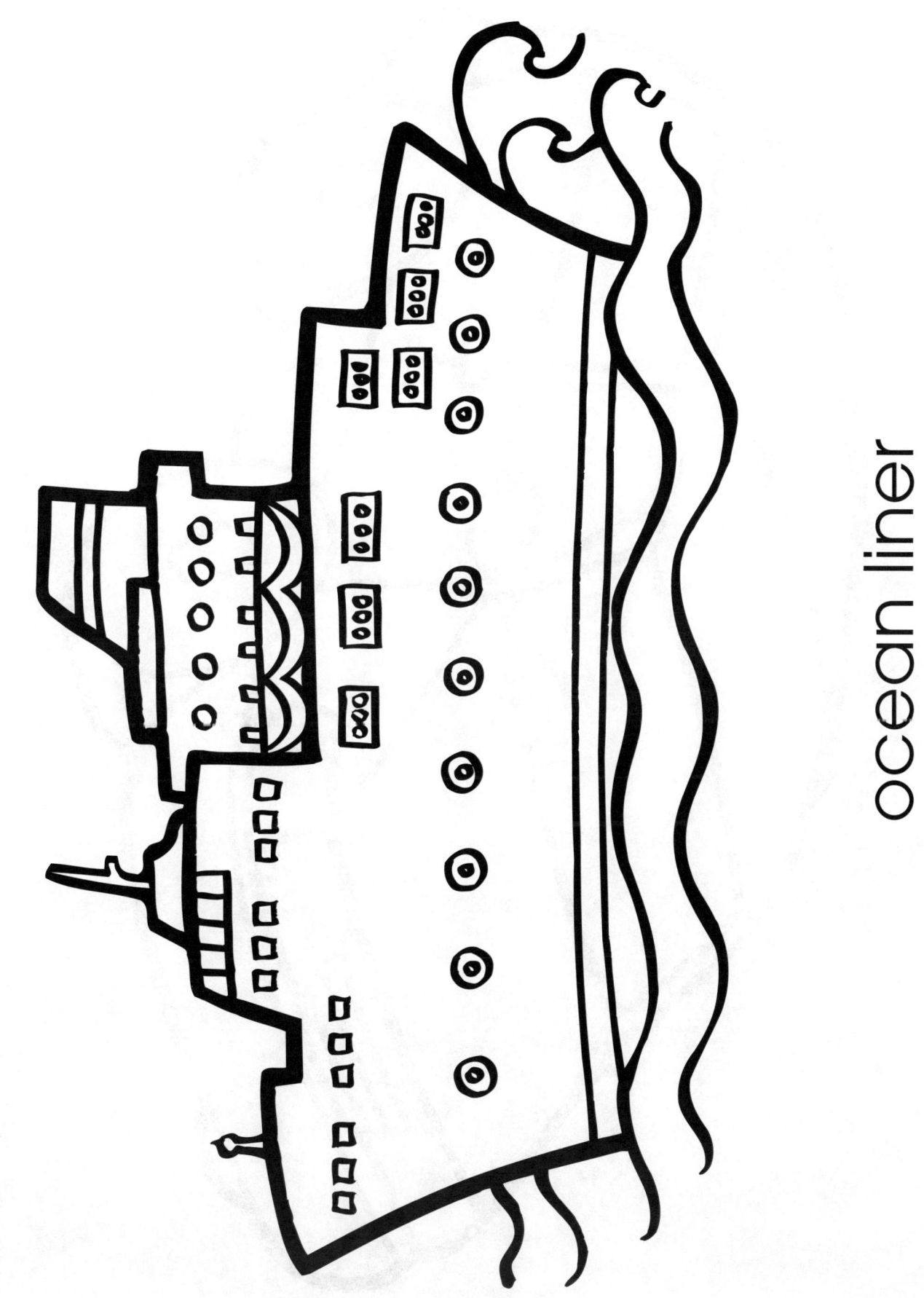

ocean liner

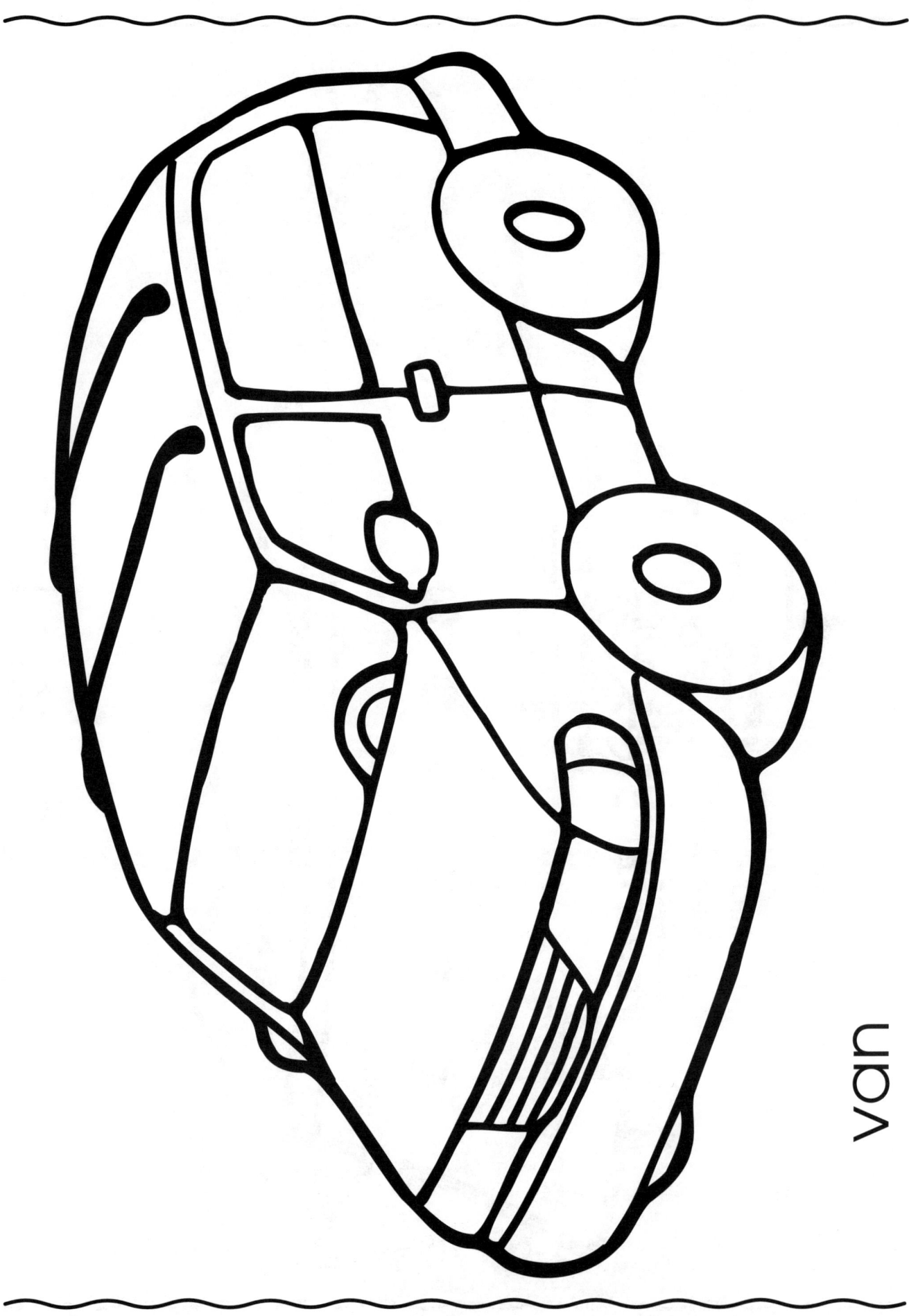

van

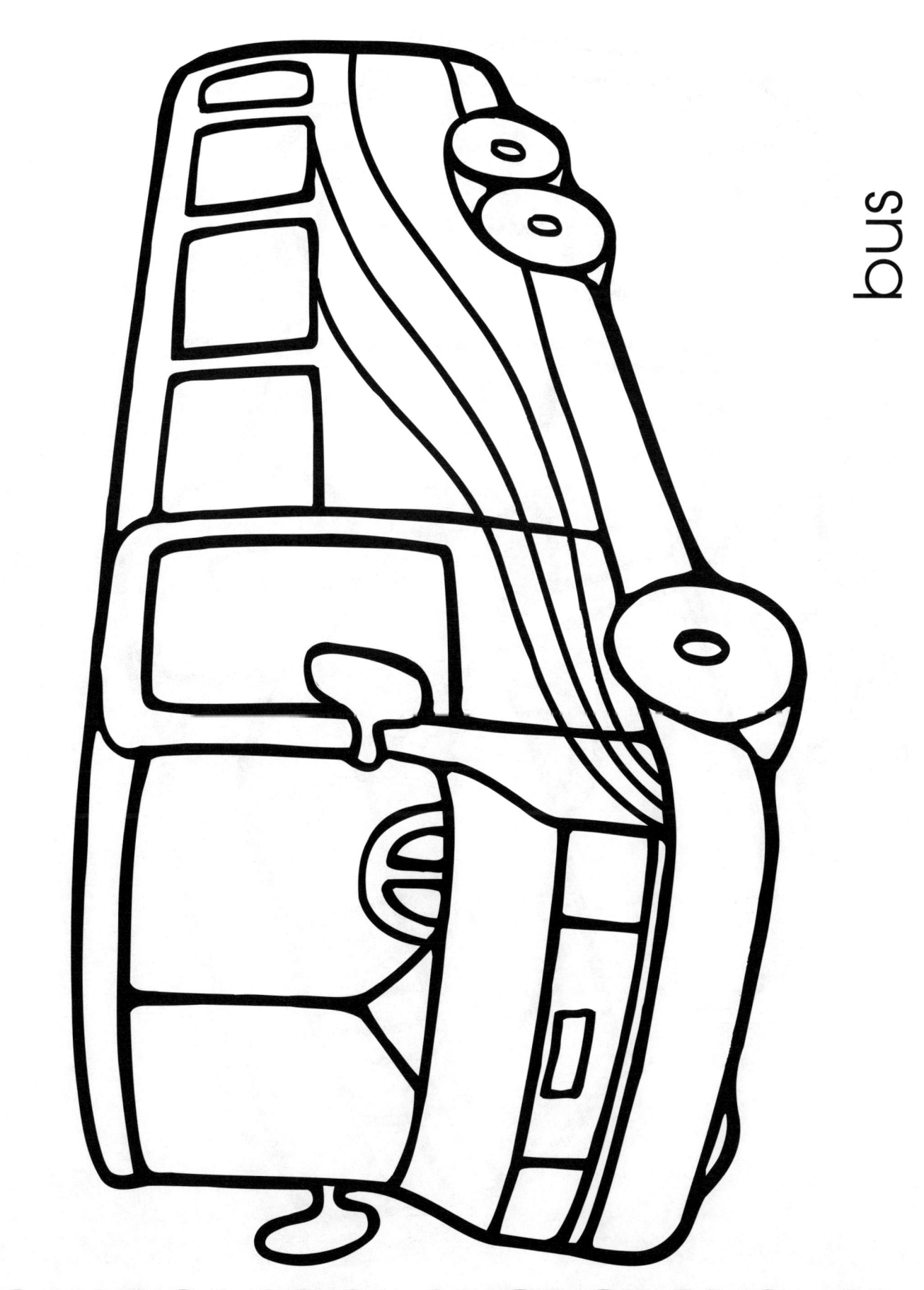
bus

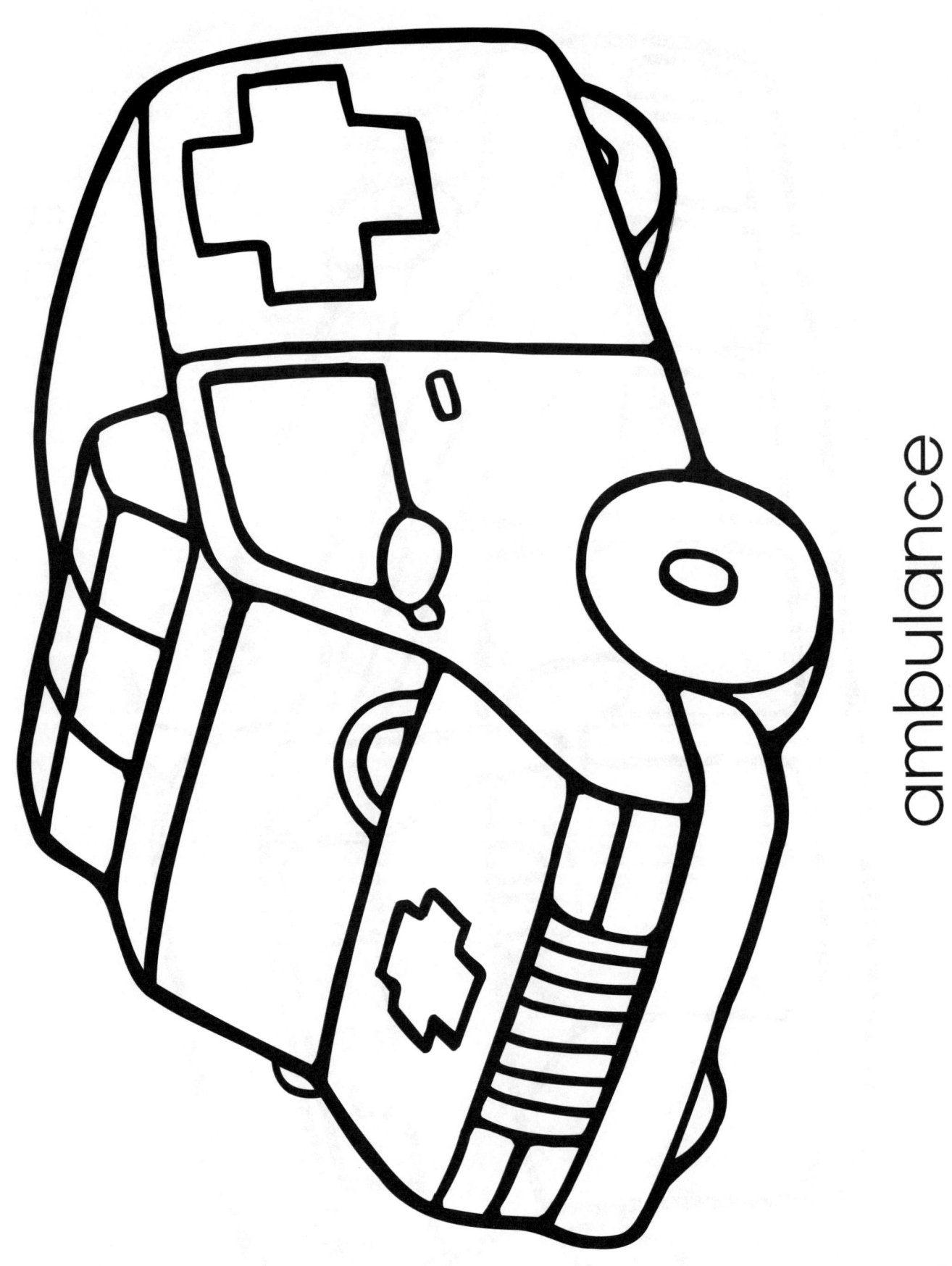

ambulance

I Know My Nursery Rhymes

Hickory, Dickory, Dock

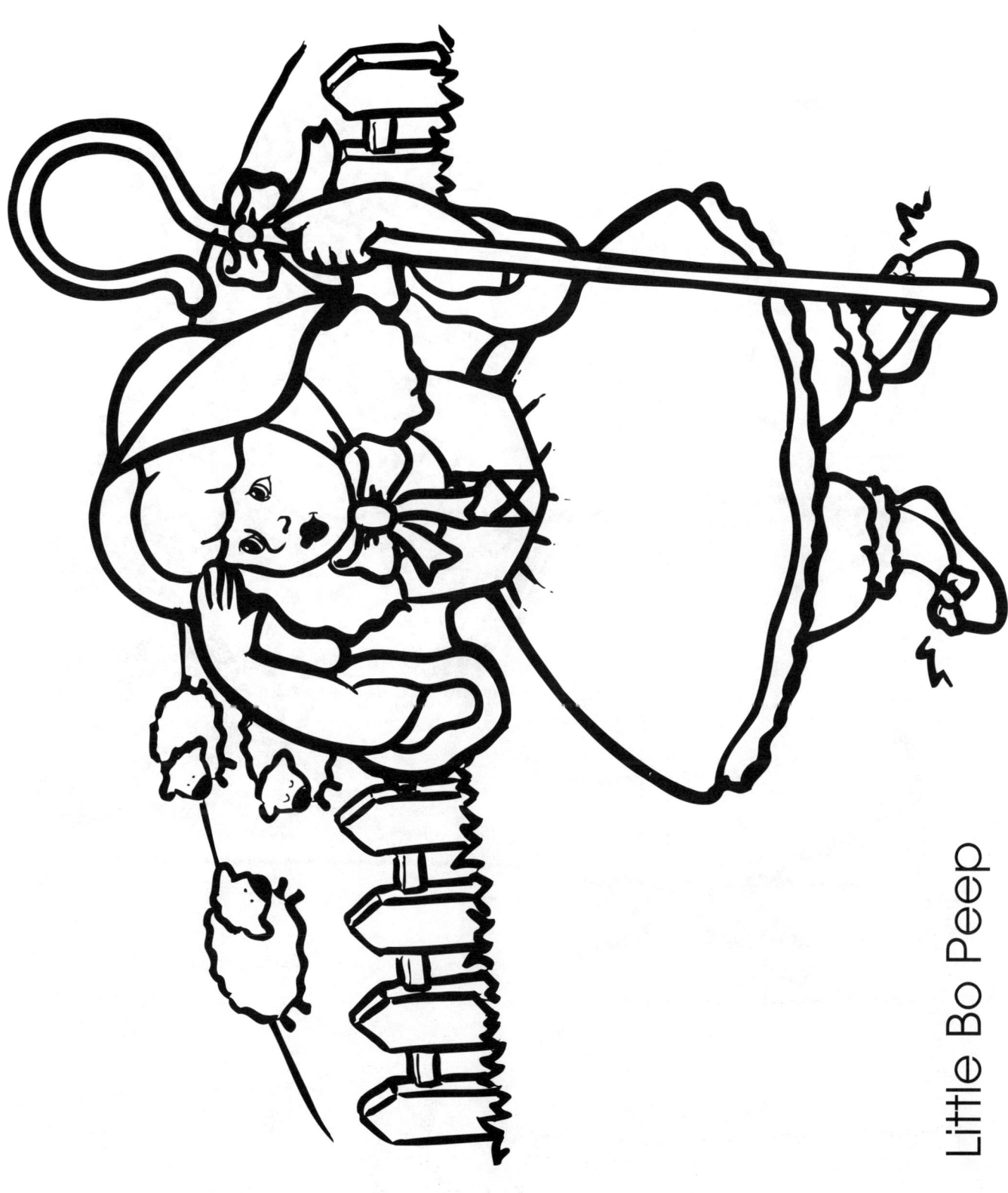
Little Bo Peep

Mary, Mary, Quite Contrary

Jack Be Nimble

Baa, Baa, Black Sheep

Pussy Cat, Pussy Cat

Humpty Dumpty

Little Jack Horner

Wee Willie Winkie

Old King Cole

Hey Diddle Diddle

Jack and Jill

Old Mother Hubbard

Sing-a-Song of Six Pence

It's Raining

1

2 # My Number Book

3

1 One

Color "1" duck.

Print the numeral "1."

Circle all the "1's."

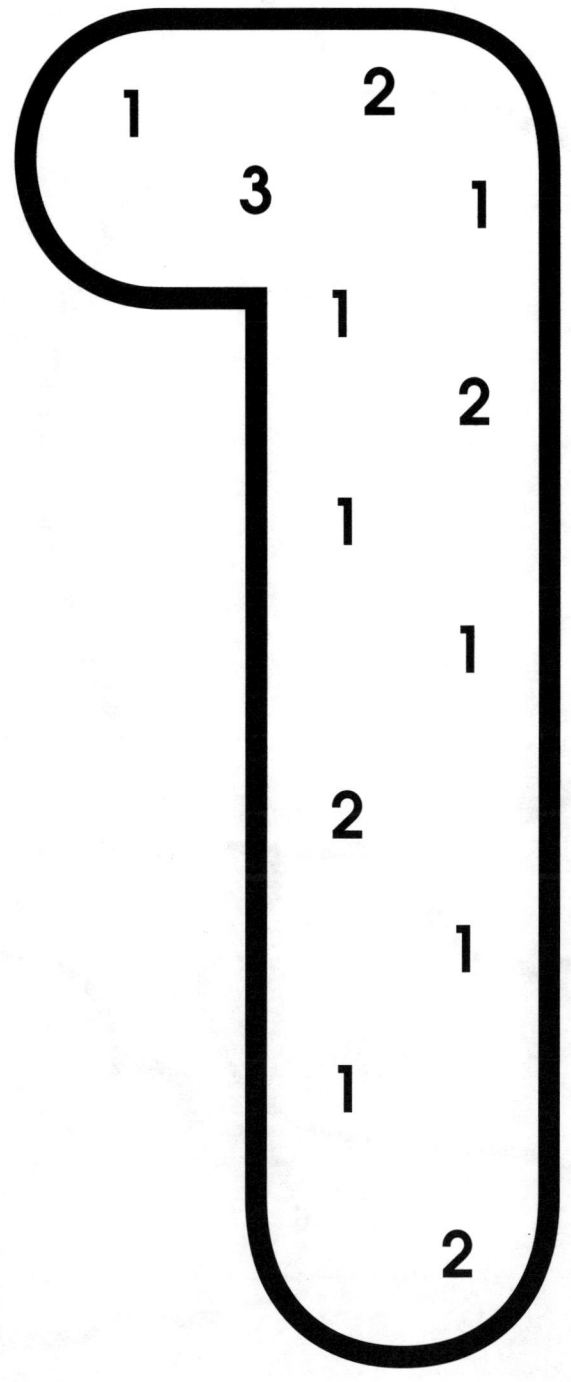

Color 1 balloon.

How many in each box?

2 Two

Color "2" cats.

Print the numeral "2."

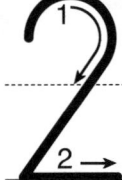

Circle all the "2's."

Color 2 bunnies.

Color, cut, and paste 2 frogs on the lily pad.

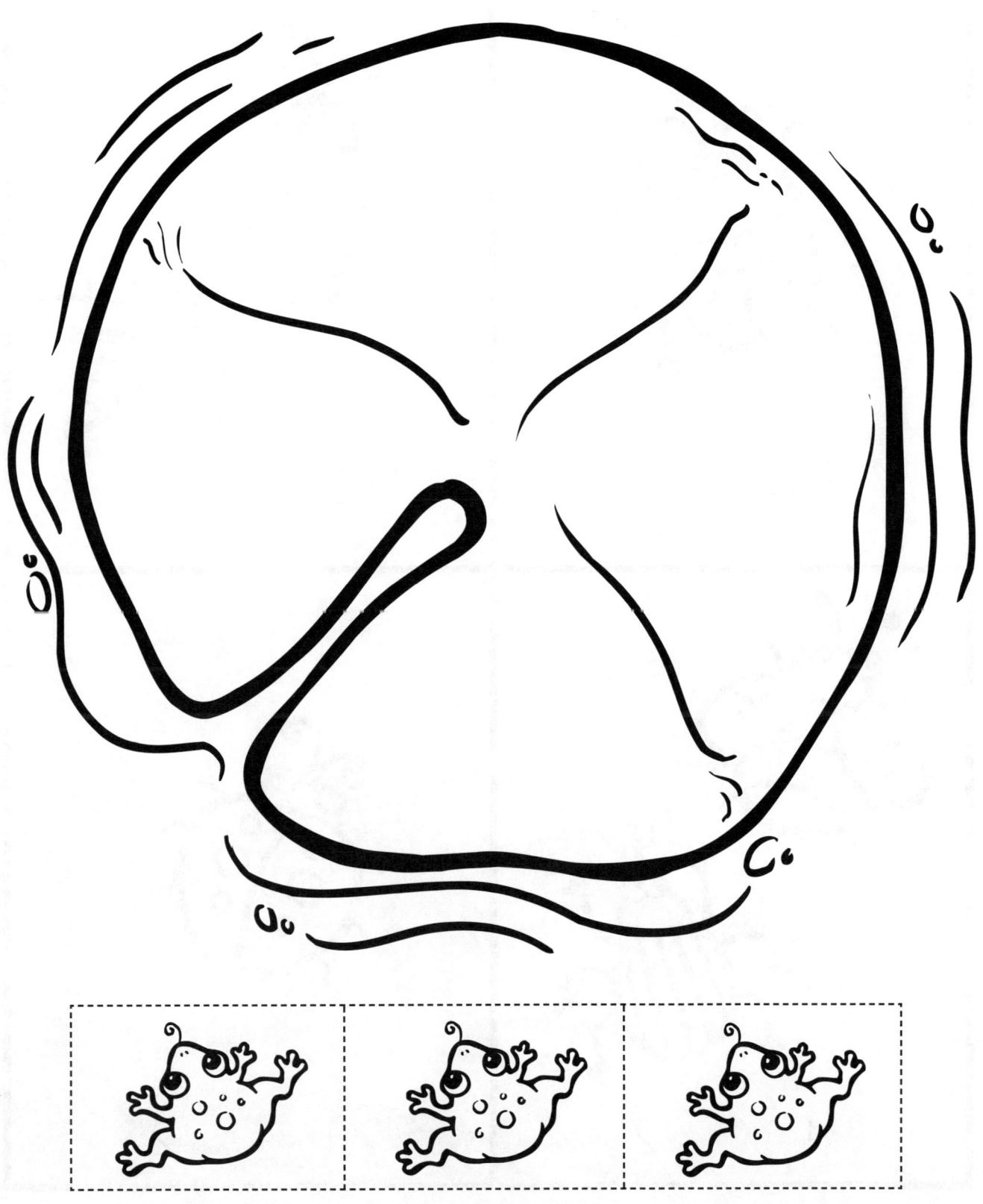

How many in each box?

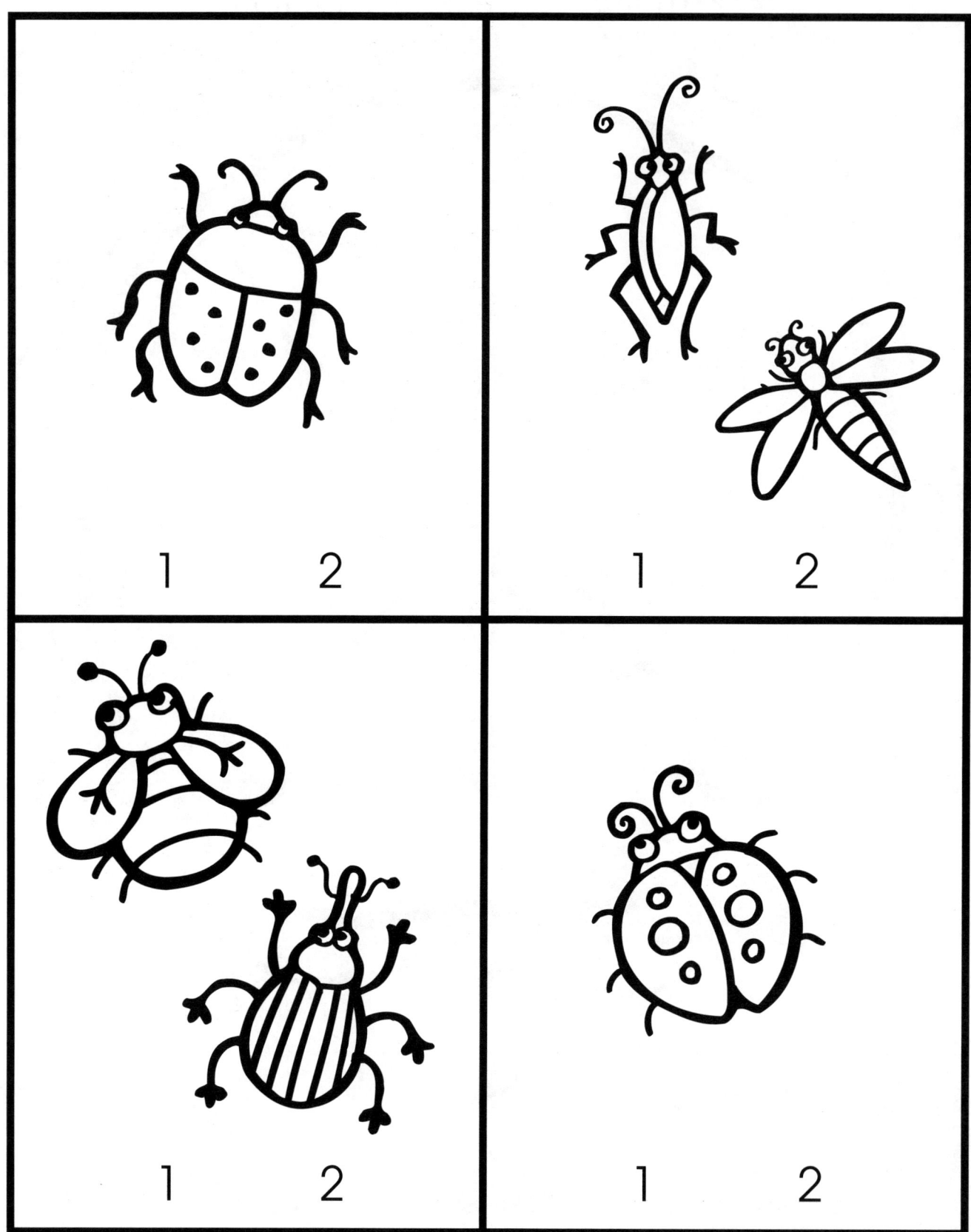

3 Three

Color "3" dogs.

Print the numeral "3."

Circle all the "3's."

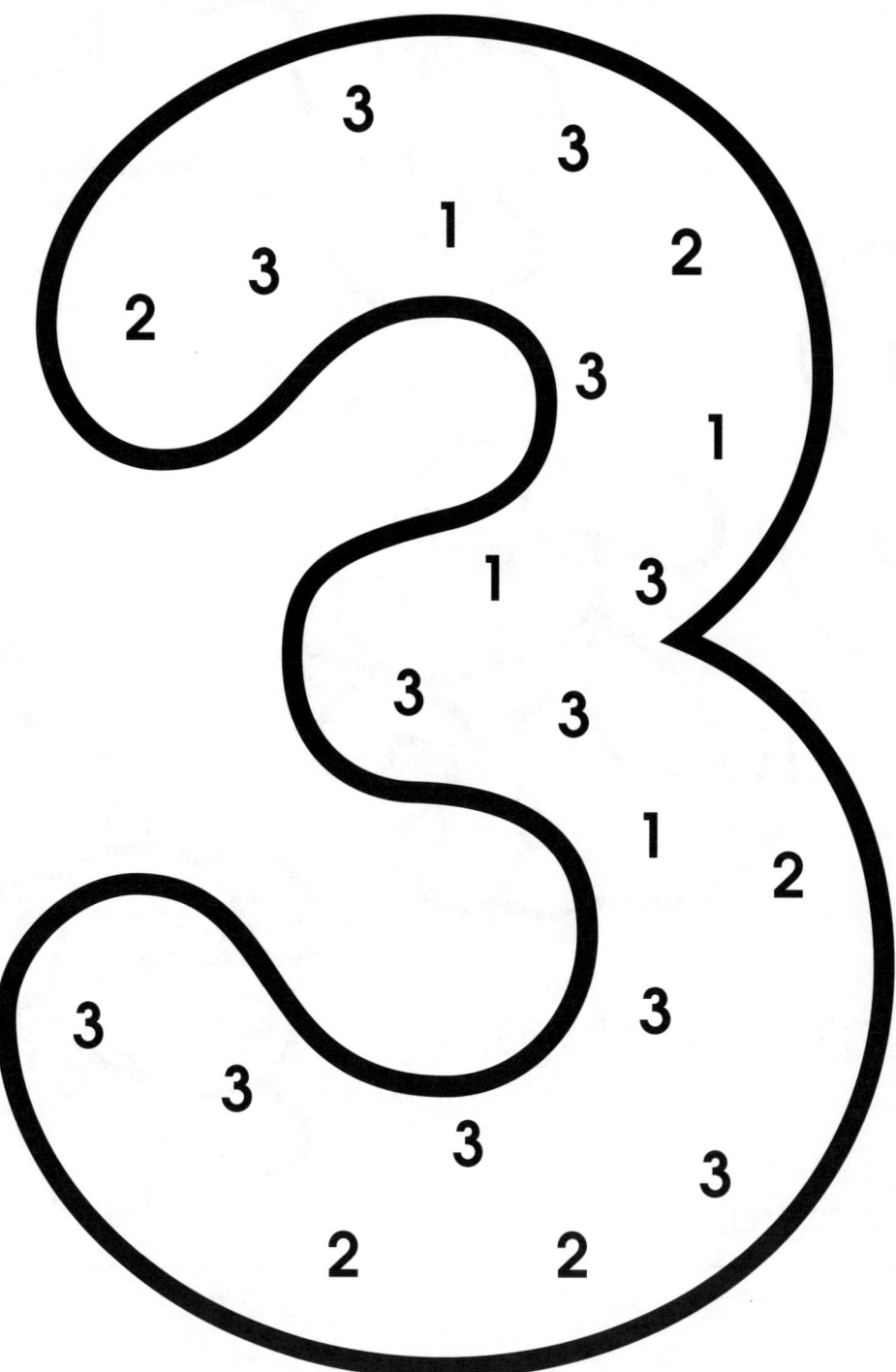

Color 3 balls.

Color, cut, and paste
3 bears in the den.

How many in each box?

Color by number.

Color 1 red.
Color 2 yellow.
Color 3 blue.

4 Four

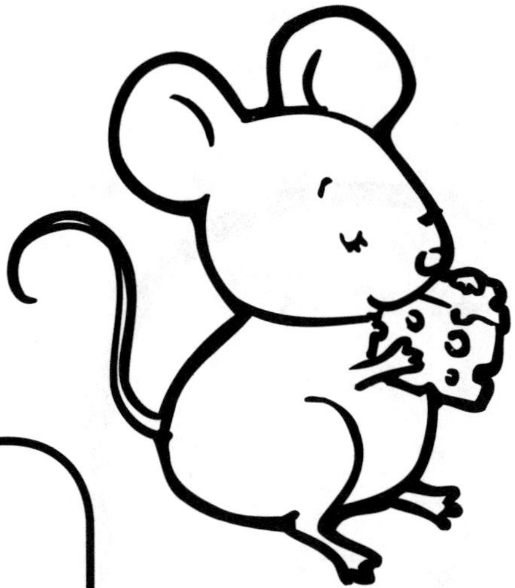

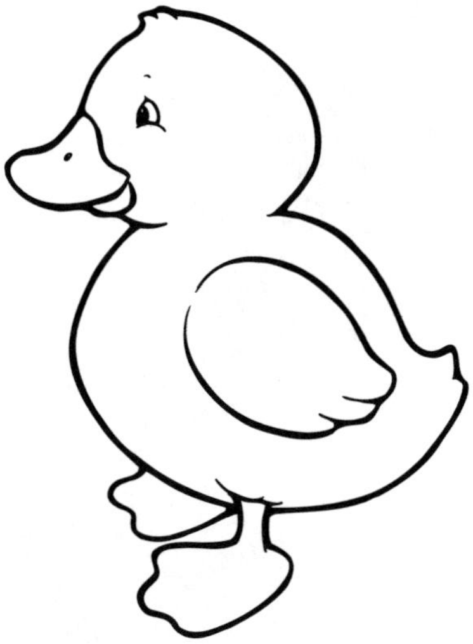

4

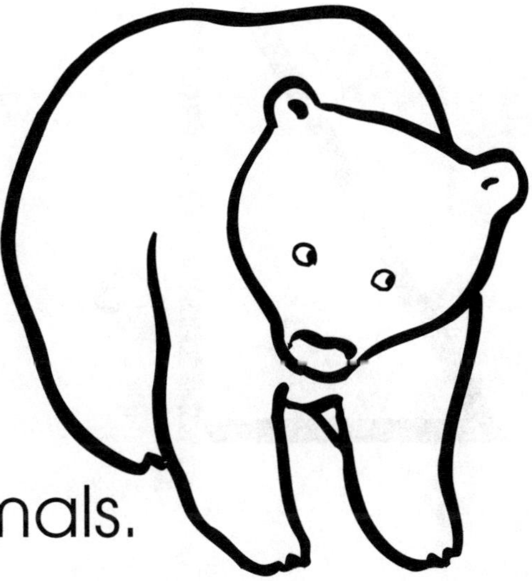

Color "4" animals.

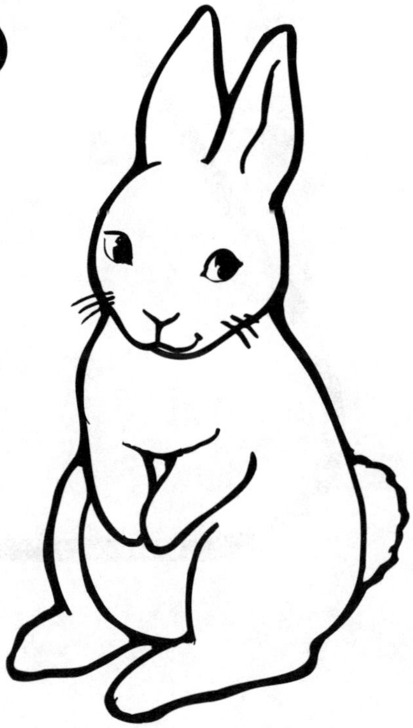

Print the numeral "4."

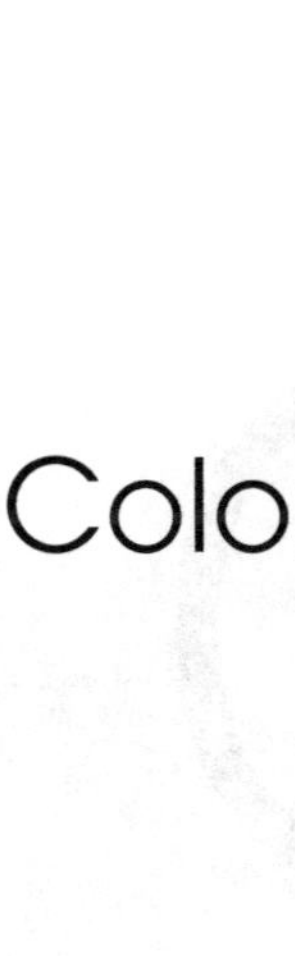

Circle all the "4's."

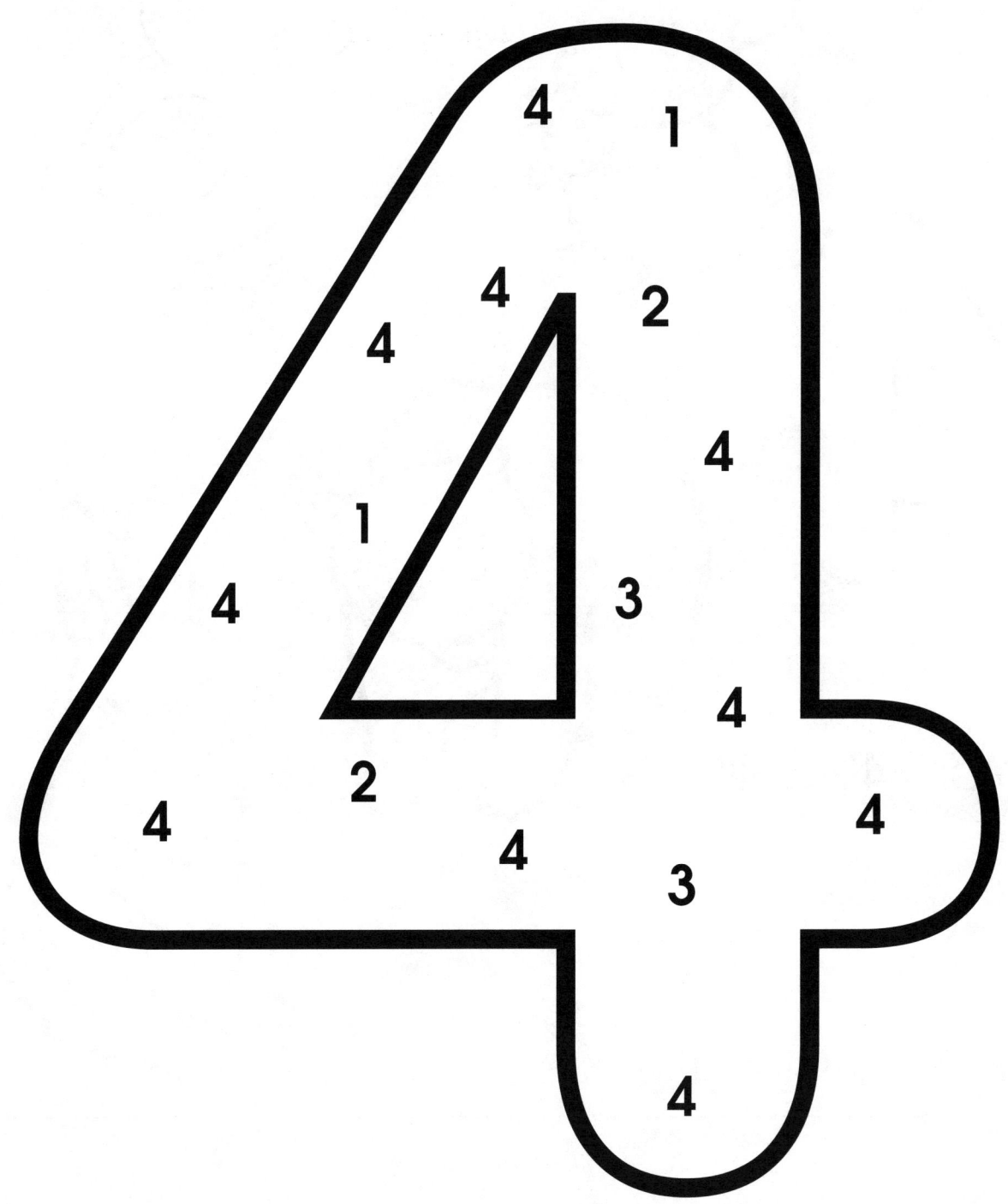

Color 4 mice.

Color, cut, and paste 4 mice in the meadow.

How many in each box?

Color by number.

Color 1 yellow.
Color 2 red.

Color 3 white.
Color 4 blue.

Dot-to-Dot
1 to 4

5 Five

Color "5" chicks.

Print the numeral "5."

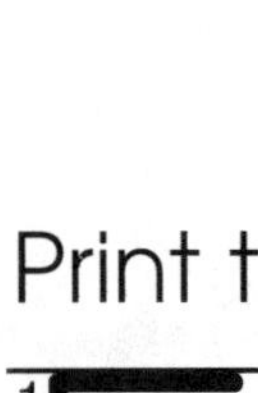

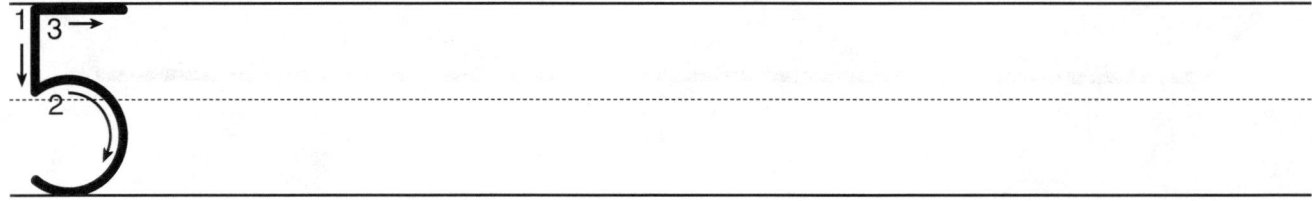

Circle all the "5's."

Color 5 kites.

Color, cut, and paste 5 dolls in a dollhouse.

 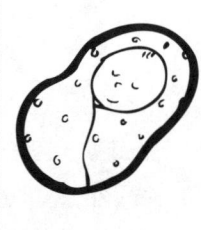    

How many in each box?

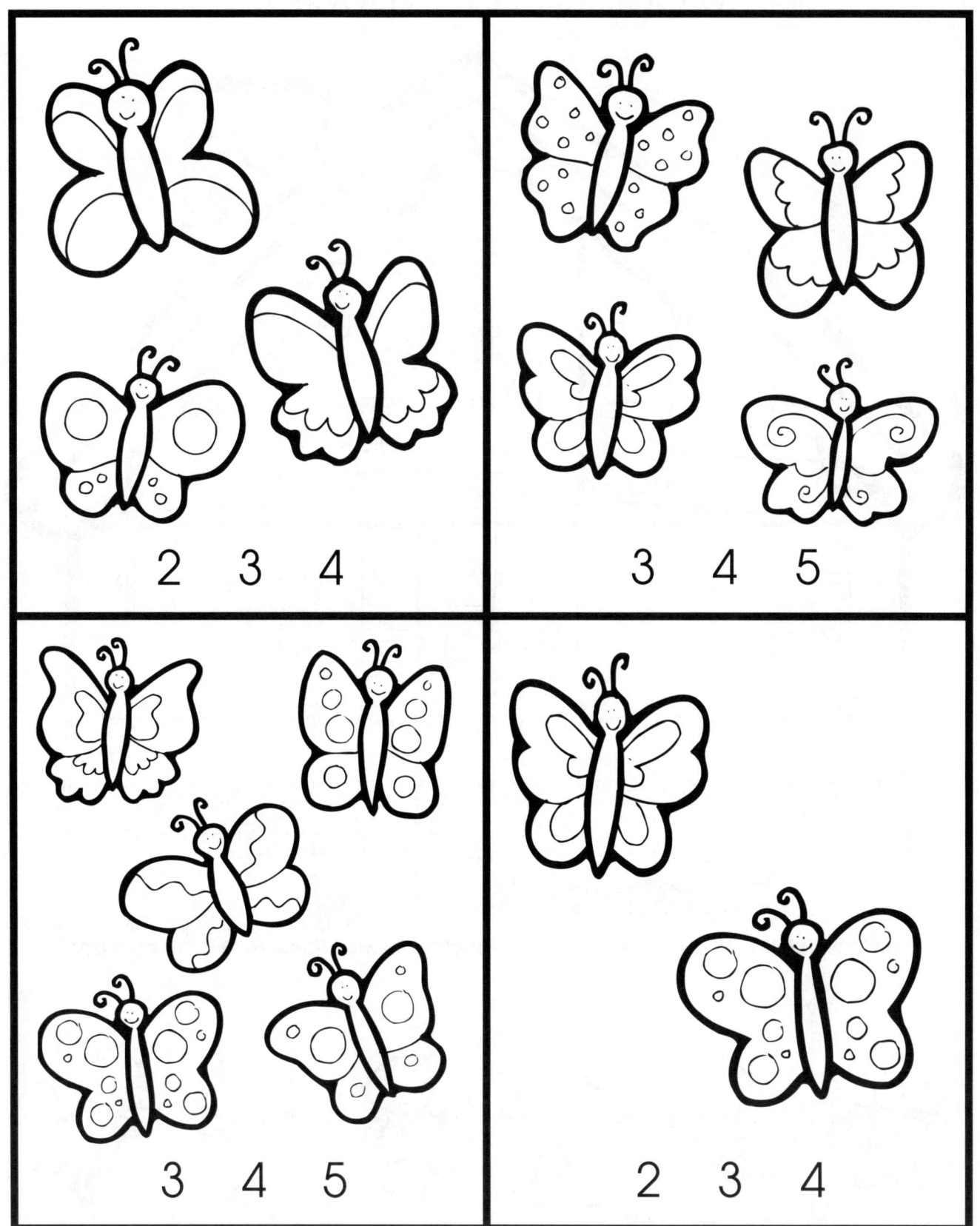

Color by number.

Color 1 yellow.
Color 2 purple.
Color 3 green.

Color 4 red.
Color 5 blue.

Dot-to-Dot
1 to 5

6 Six

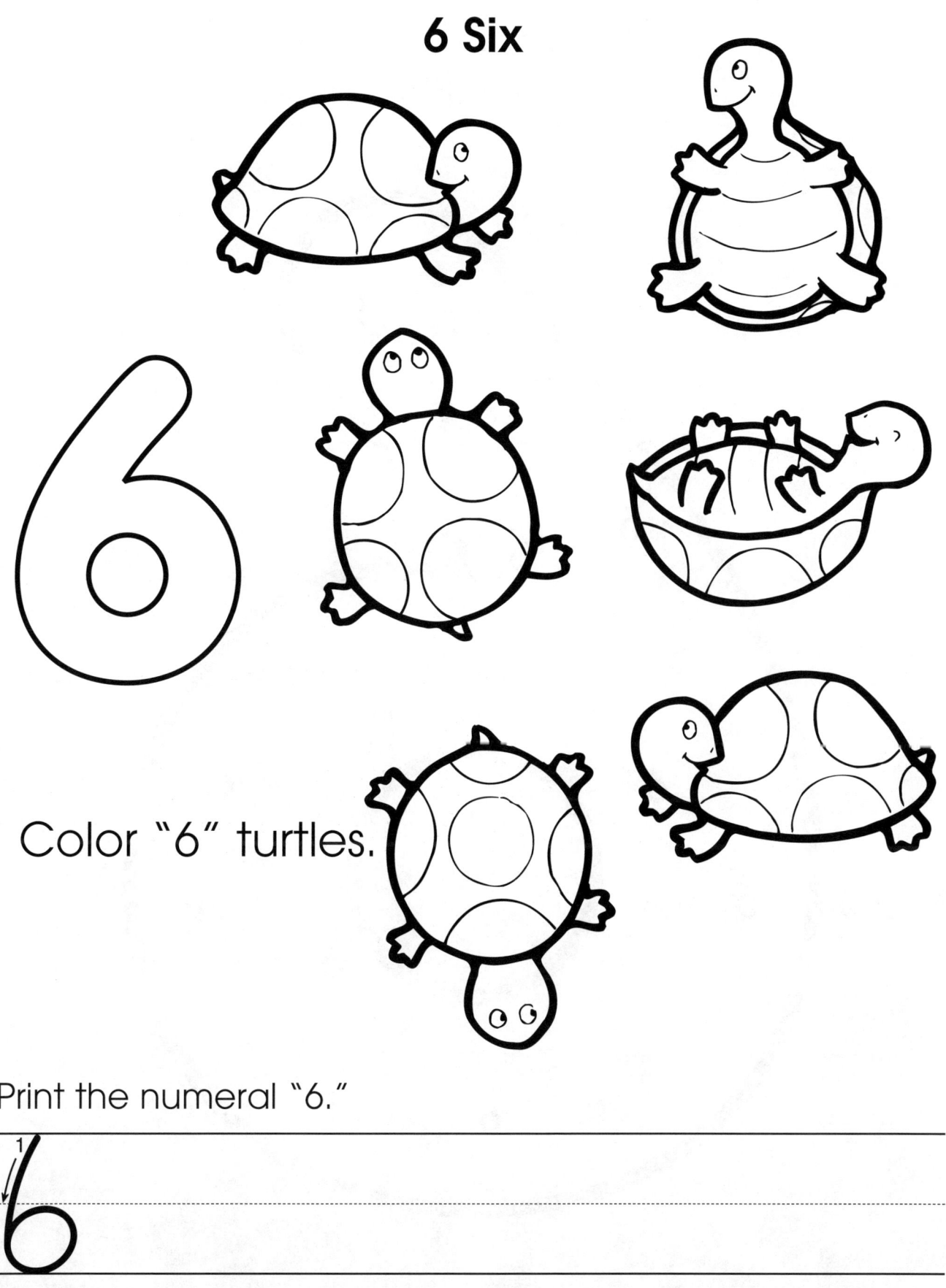

Color "6" turtles.

Print the numeral "6."

Circle all the "6's."

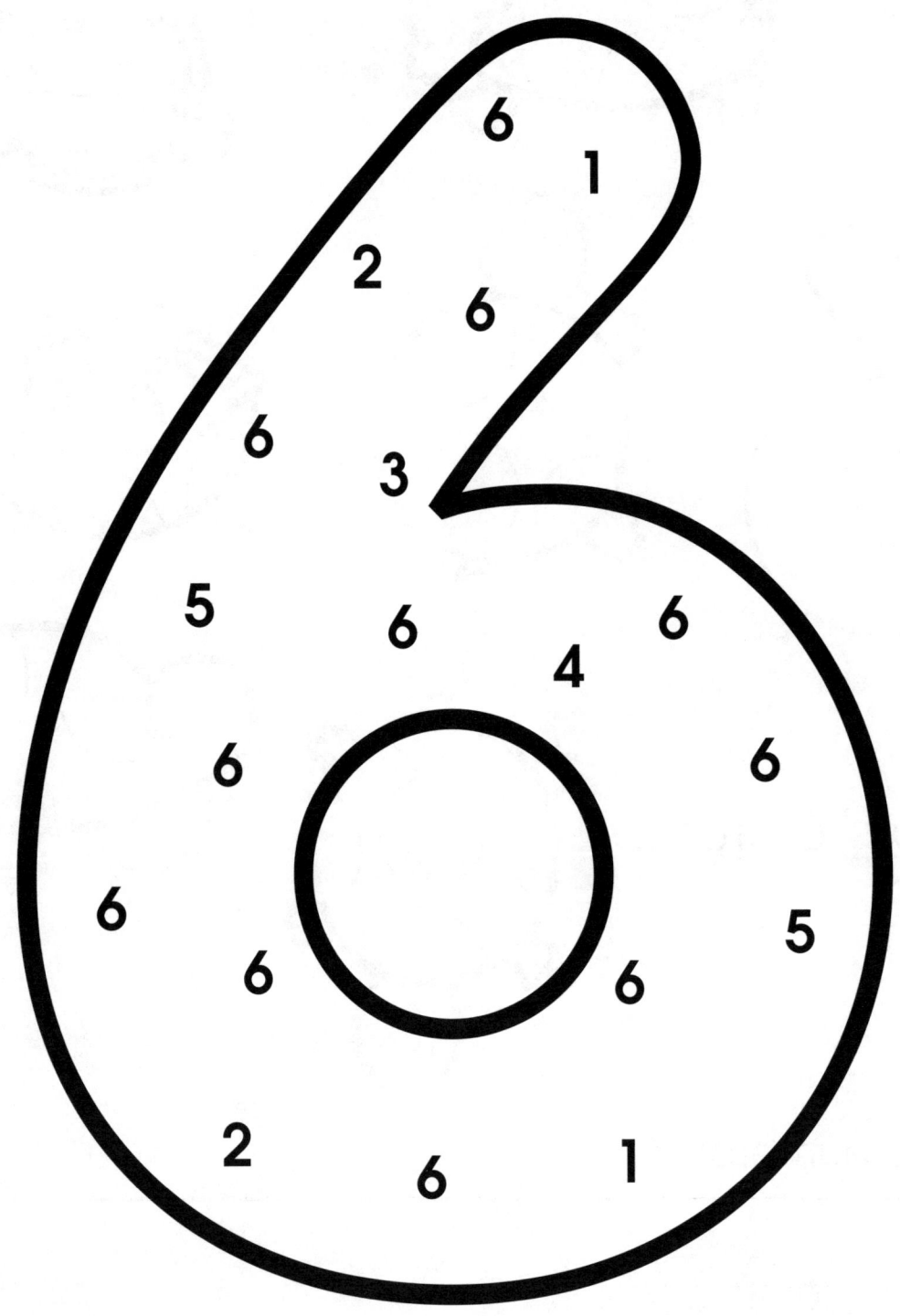

Color 6 frogs.

How many in each box?

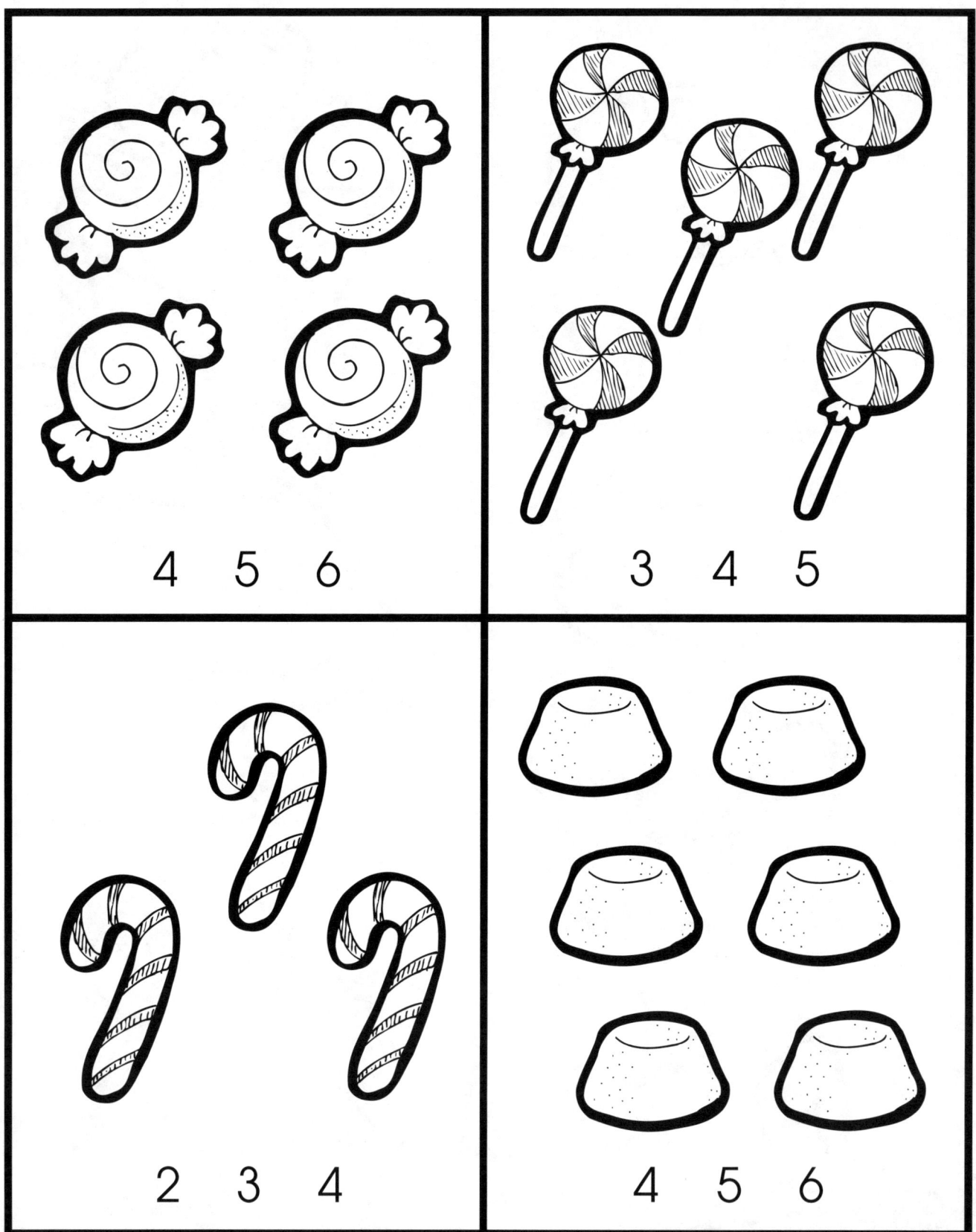

Color by number.

Color 1 brown.
Color 2 yellow.
Color 3 orange.

Color 4 blue.
Color 5 red.
Color 6 green.

Dot-to-Dot
1 to 6

7 Seven

Color "7" butterflies.

Print the numeral "7."

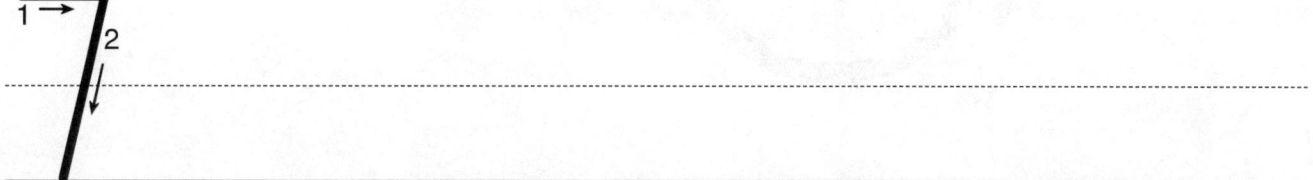

Circle all the "7's."

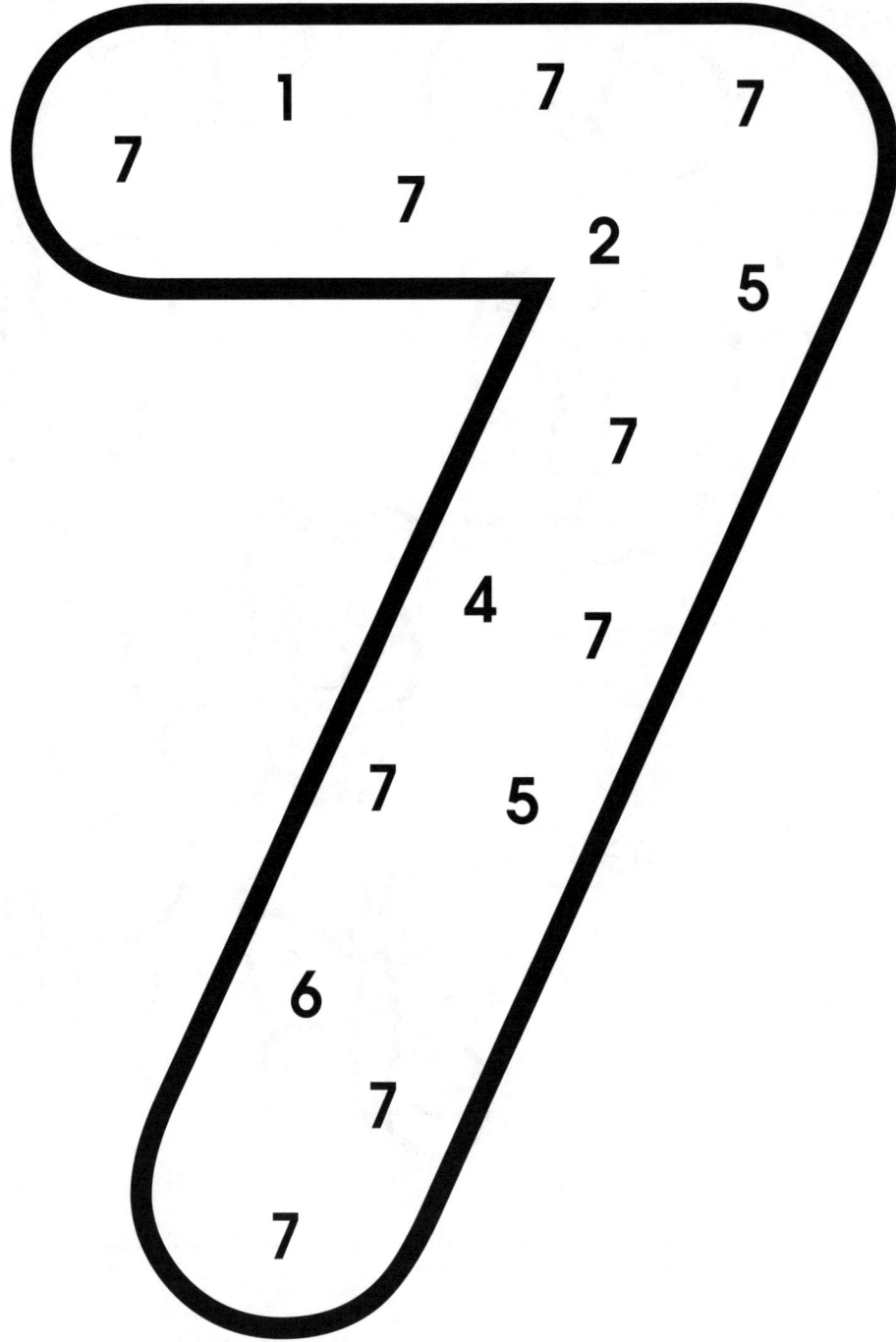

Color 7 fish.

How many in each box?

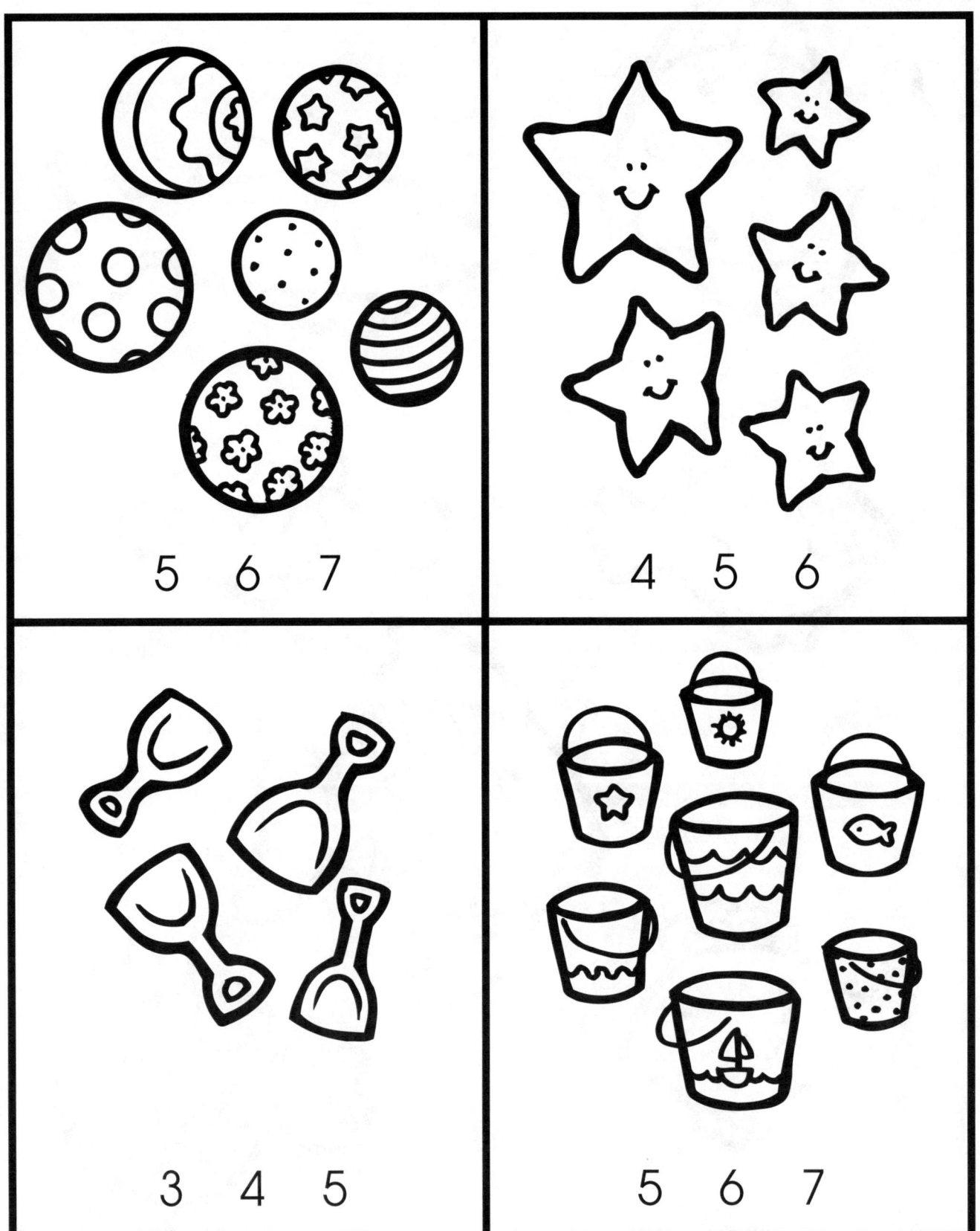

Color by number.

Color 1 yellow.
Color 2 purple.
Color 3 brown.
Color 4 green.

Color 5 blue.
Color 6 red.
Color 7 orange.

Dot-to-Dot
1 to 7

Match the numeral to the set.
Draw a line.

1 ♡ ♡ ♡ ♡

2 ☺ ☺ ☺ ☺ ☺ ☺

3 ✿ ✿

4 🐻 🐻 🐻 🐻 🐻 🐻 🐻

5 🦋

6 🍃 🍃 🍃

7 ☆ ☆ ☆ ☆ ☆

8 Eight

Color "8" bees.

Print the numeral "8."

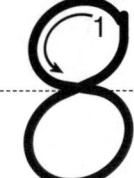

Circle all the "8's."

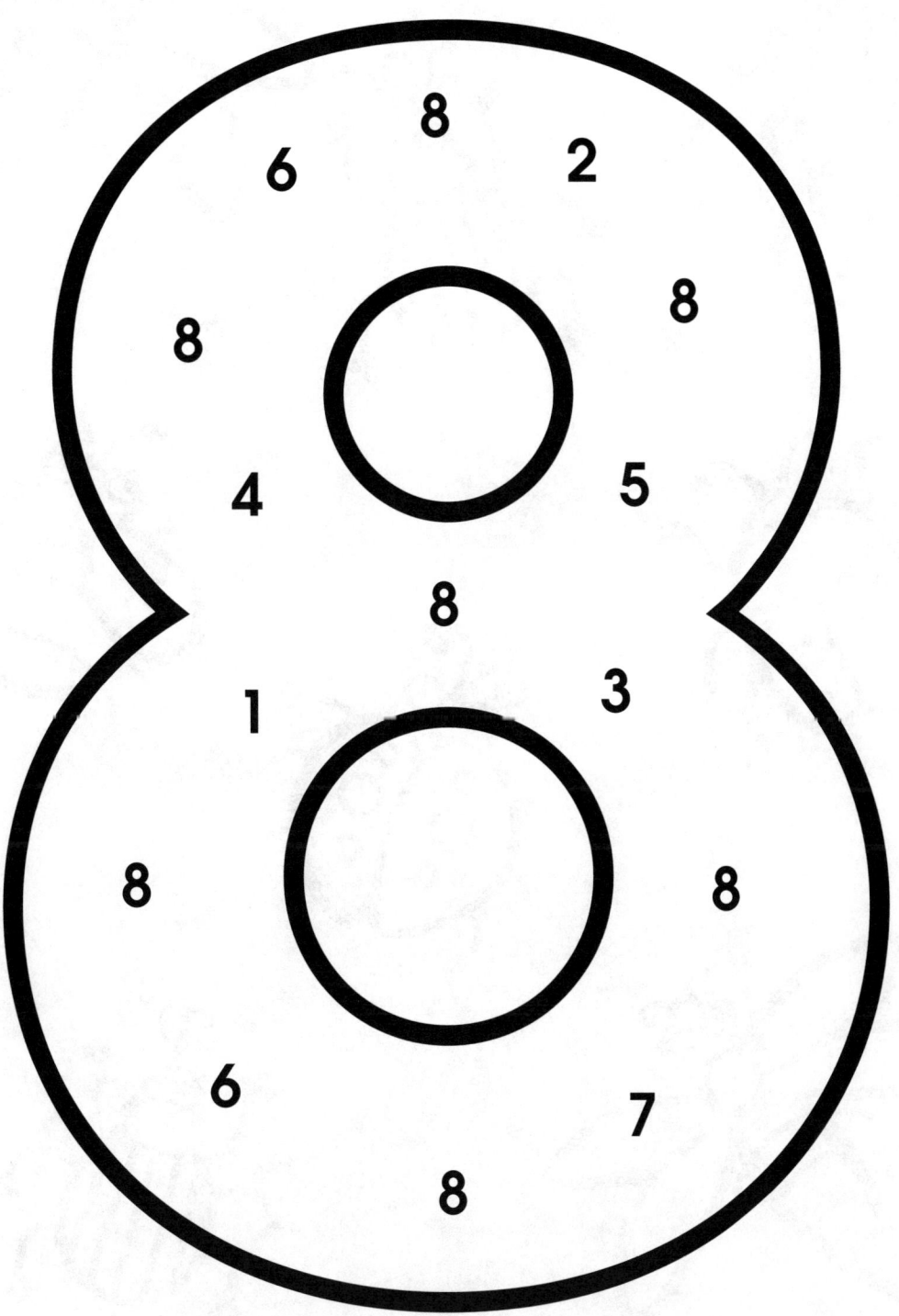

Color 8 bugs.

How many in each box?

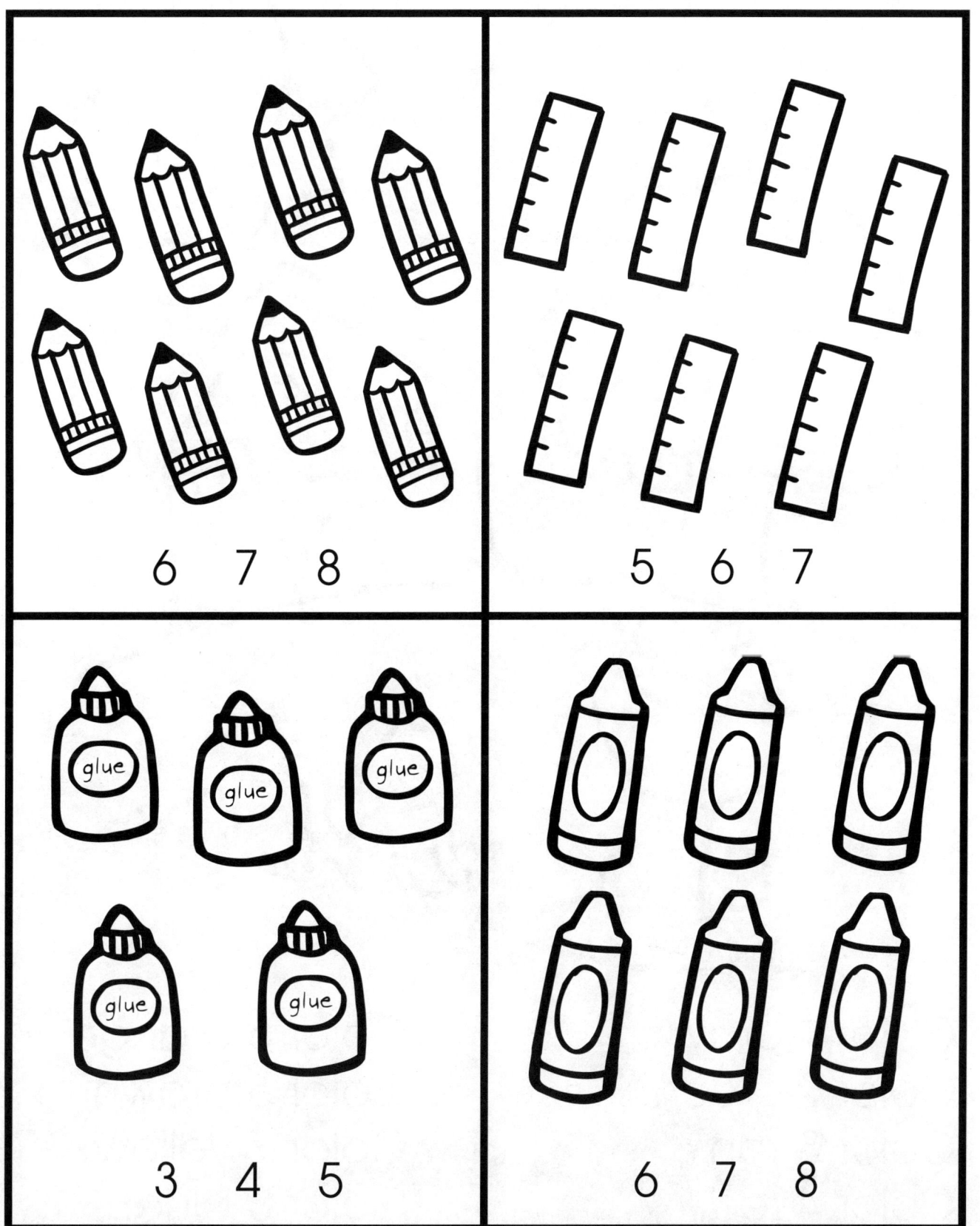

Color by number.

Color 1 gray.
Color 2 green.
Color 3 tan.
Color 4 red.

Color 5 orange.
Color 6 brown.
Color 7 yellow.
Color 8 blue.

Dot-to-Dot
1 to 8

Match the numeral to the set. Draw a line.

1 ♡ ♡ ♡ ♡ ♡

2 ☆ ☆

3 ☺

4 ꕥ ꕥ ꕥ ꕥ ꕥ ꕥ ꕥ

5 ☐ ☐ ☐

6 🐻 🐻 🐻 🐻

7 🍃 🍃 🍃 🍃 🍃 🍃 🍃 🍃

8 🦋 🦋 🦋 🦋 🦋 🦋

8 Eight

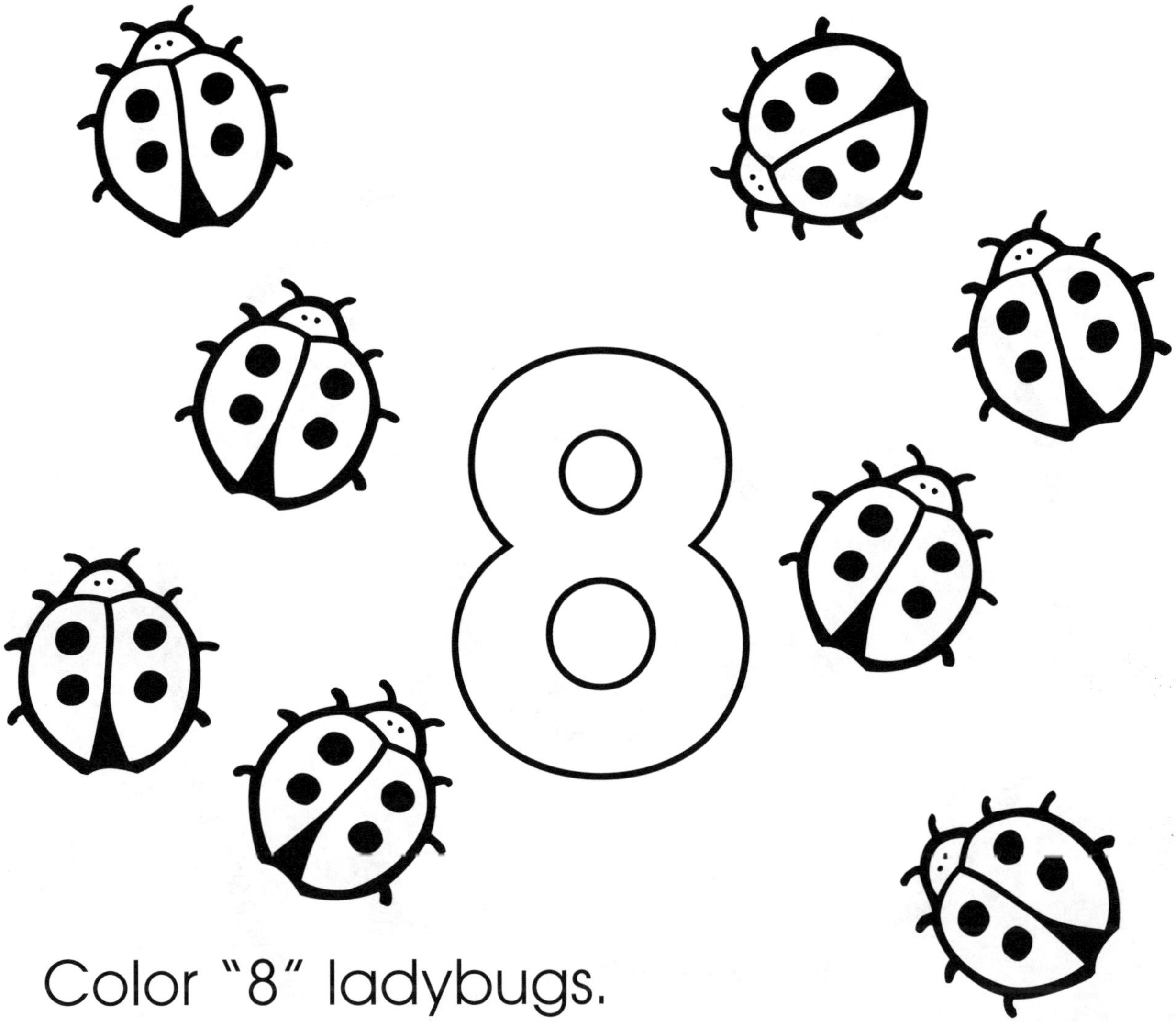

Color "8" ladybugs.

Print the numeral "8."

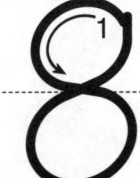

Circle all the "9's."

Color 9 cars.

How many in each box?

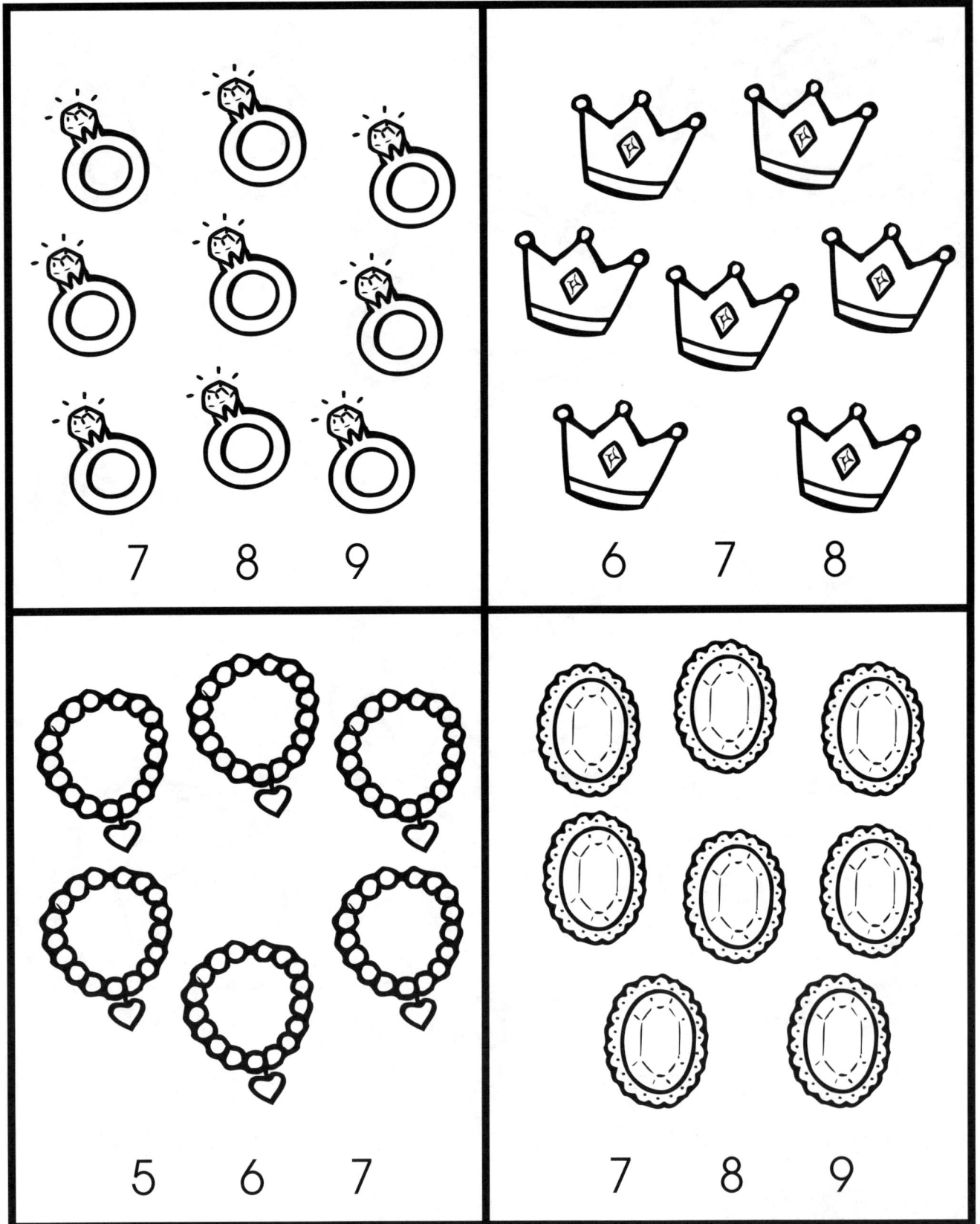

Color by number.

Color 1 tan.
Color 2 brown.
Color 3 orange.
Color 4 green.
Color 5 red.

Color 6 purple.
Color 7 pink.
Color 8 blue.
Color 9 yellow.

Dot-to-Dot
1 to 9

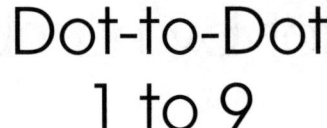

Match the numeral to the set.
Draw a line.

1

2

3

4

5

6

7

8

9

10 Ten

Color "10" chipmunks.

Print the numeral "10."

Circle all the "10's."

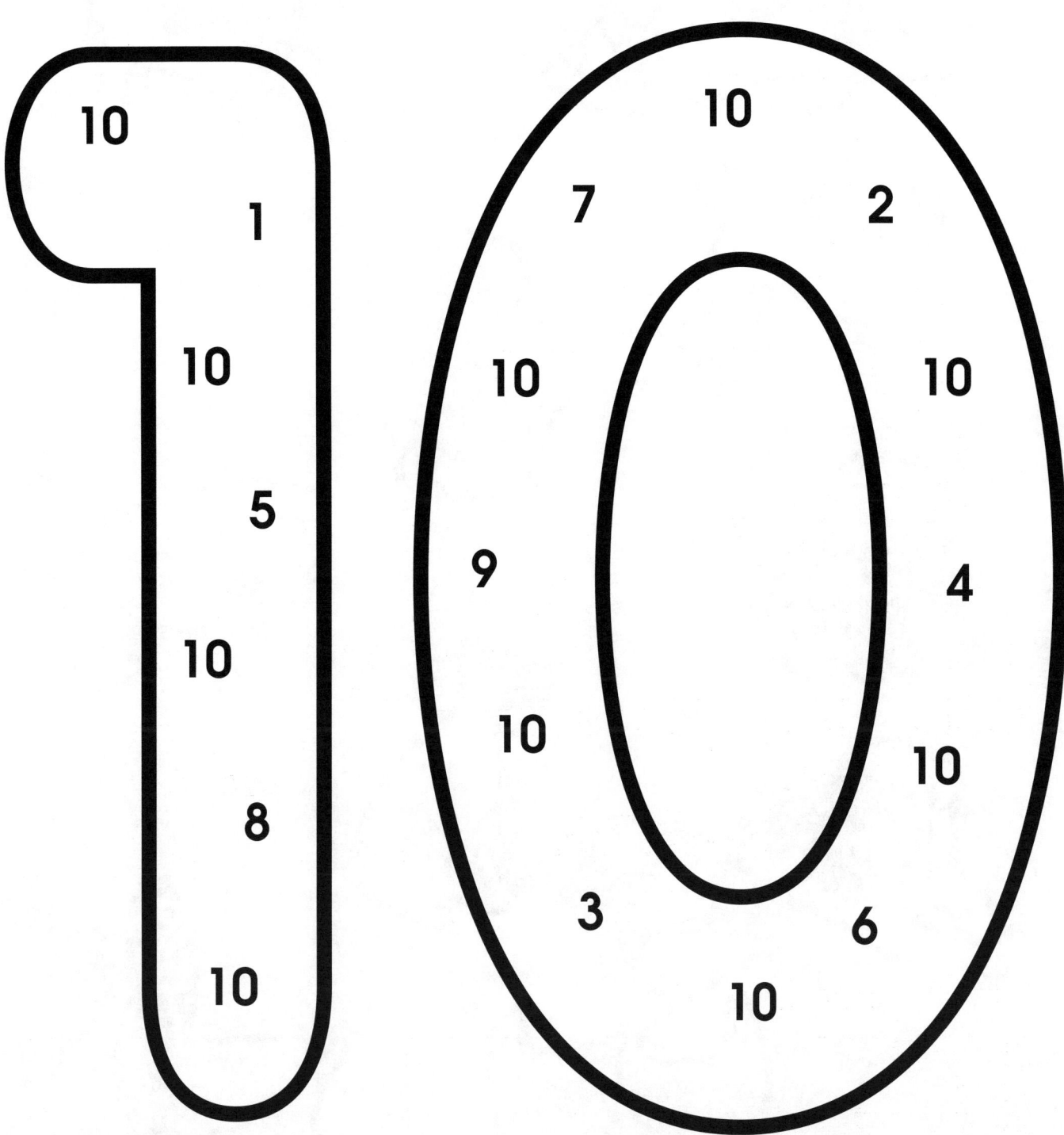

Color 10 puppies.

Color, cut, and paste 10 ladybugs on the leaf.

How many in each box?

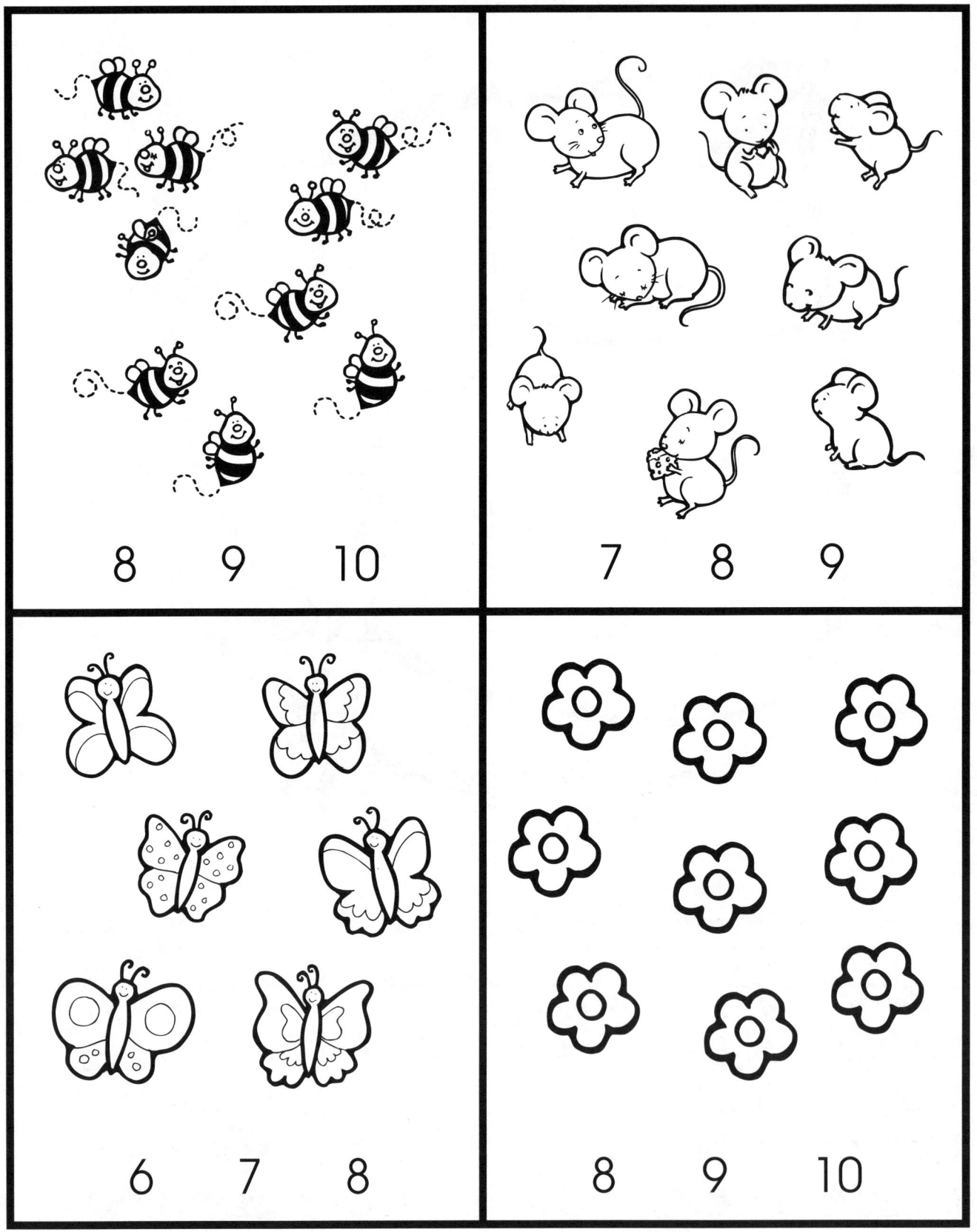

Color by number.

Color 1 red.
Color 2 yellow.
Color 3 blue.
Color 4 green.
Color 5 orange.

Color 6 purple.
Color 7 black.
Color 8 brown.
Color 9 pink.
Color 10 gray.

Dot-to-Dot
1 to 10

Let's Learn About the Weather

The sun is warm.

Rain is wet.

Snow is cold.

The wind can be chilly.

We dress this way on a rainy day.

We dress this way on a warm, sunny day.

We dress this way on a windy day.

We dress this way on a cold day.

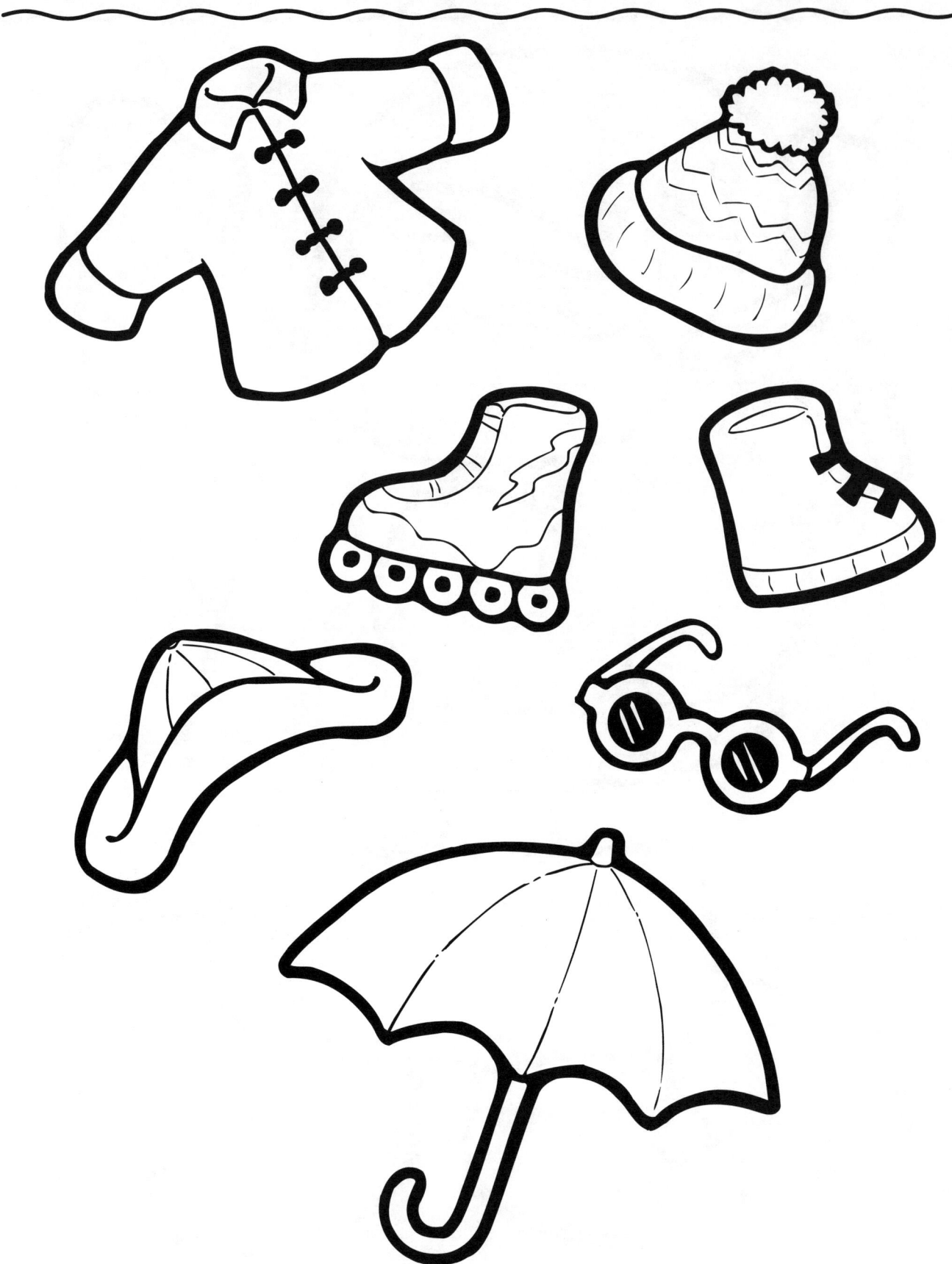

What would you wear on a rainy day?

What would you wear on a hot day?

What would you wear on a cold day?

The Farm

This is the farmer.

This is the farmer's wife.

The farmer drives a tractor.

The farmer grows food.

Many animals live in the barn.

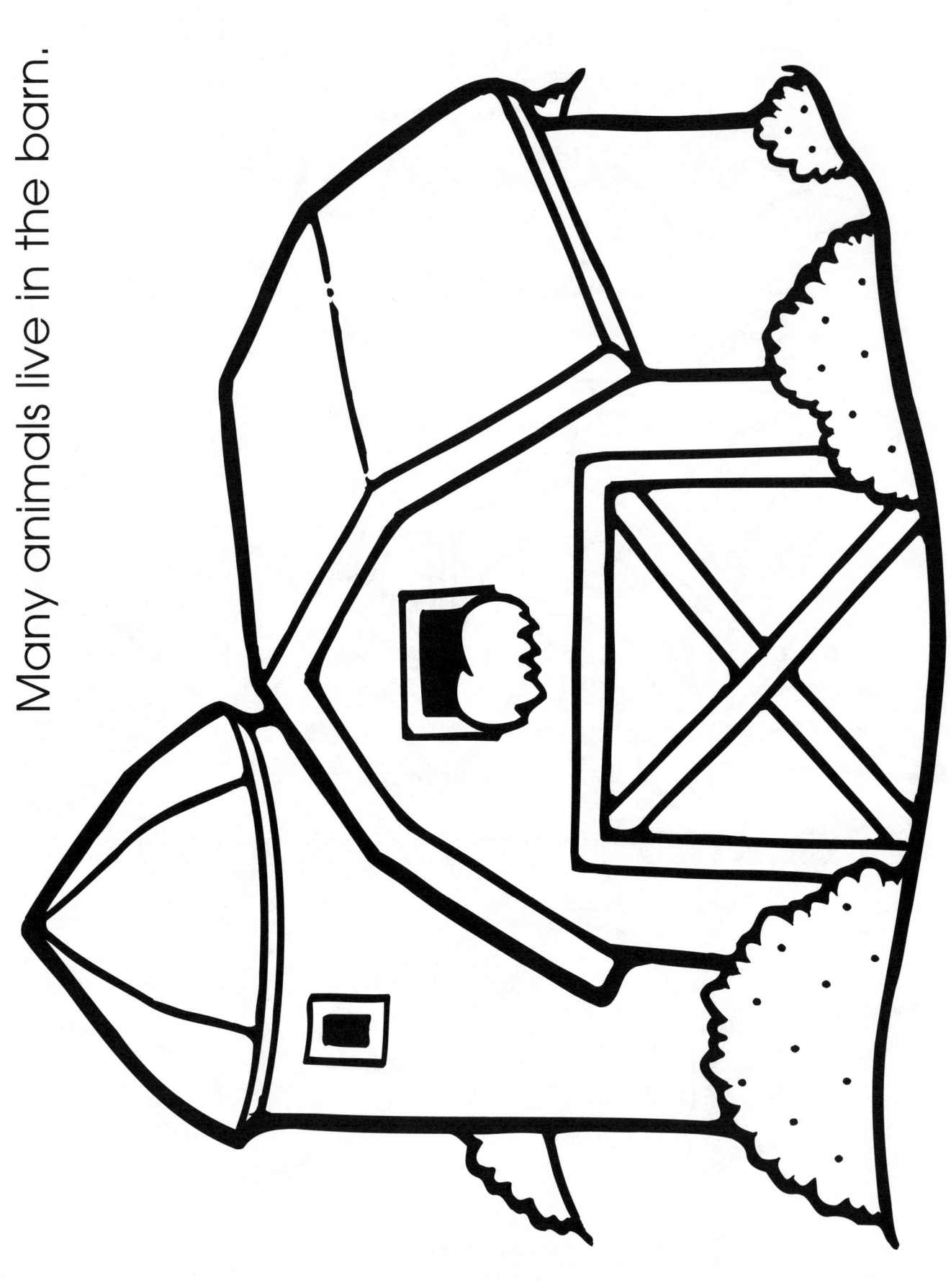

This is a cow.

This is a horse.

This is a pig.

This is a goat.

This is a duck.

This is a sheep.

This is a chicken.

This is a rooster.

These are rabbits.

These are geese.

This is a barn cat.

These are the children
who live on the farm.

Basic
Concepts

Up
Cut, paste, and color.
Put the mountain climber going "up" the mountain.

Down

Cut, paste, and color.
Put the bunny going "down" the slide.

On
Cut, paste, and color.
Put the teddy bear "on" the bed.

Off

Cut, paste, and color.
Put the lampshade on the lamp that is turned "off."

Top
Cut, paste, and color.
Put the school bell on "top" of the schoolhouse.

Bottom

Cut, paste, and color.
Put the drum on the "bottom" shelf.

Over

Cut, paste, and color.
Put the plane "over" the cloud.

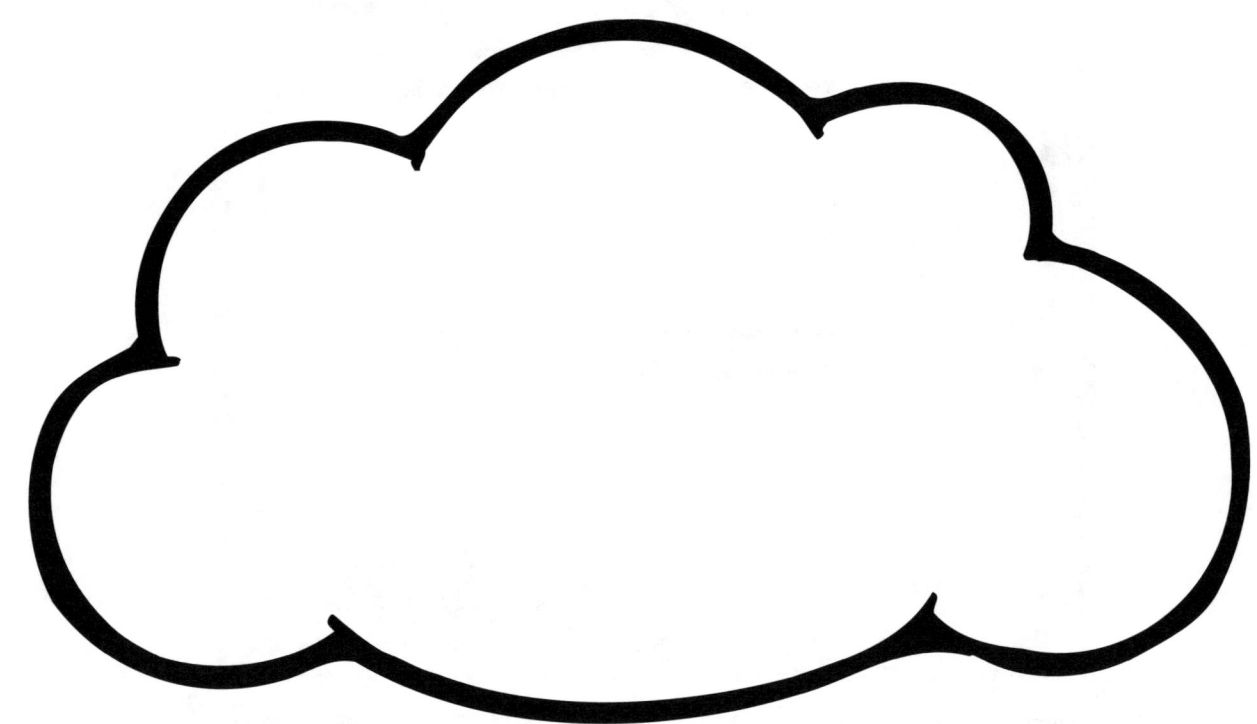

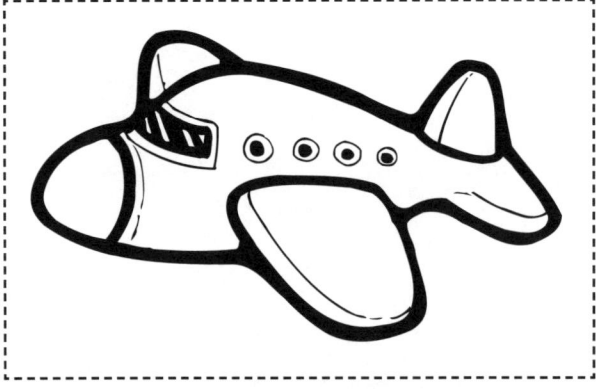

Under

Cut, paste, and color.
Put the bear "under" the beehive.

Outside

Cut, paste, and color.
Put the bat "outside" the bat cave.

Inside

Cut, paste, and color.
Put the mouse "inside" the mouse hole.

Back
Cut, paste, and color.
Put the ball into the "back" of the wagon.

Front

Cut, paste, and color.
Put the rows of flowers in the "front" of the house.

Above

Cut, paste, and color.
Put the spaceship "above" the stars.

Below

Cut, paste, and color.
Put the rocket "below" the moon.

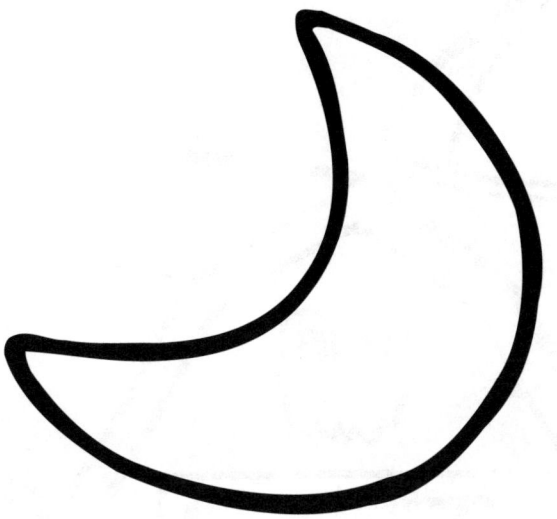

Beside

Cut, paste, and color.
Put the chicken "beside" the barn.

Between

Cut, paste, and color.
Put the basket of fruit "between" the trees.

Behind

Cut, paste, and color.
Put the cart "behind" the horse.

My Alphabet Book

Aa **Bb** **Cc**

Letter "Aa"

Color the uppercase letters red.
Color the lowercase letters blue.

Color the pictures that begin with **A**.

Letter "Bb"

Color the uppercase letters red.
Color the lowercase letters blue.

Color the pictures that begin with **B**.

Letter "Cc"

Color the uppercase letters green.
Color the lowercase letters yellow.

Color the pictures that begin with **C**.

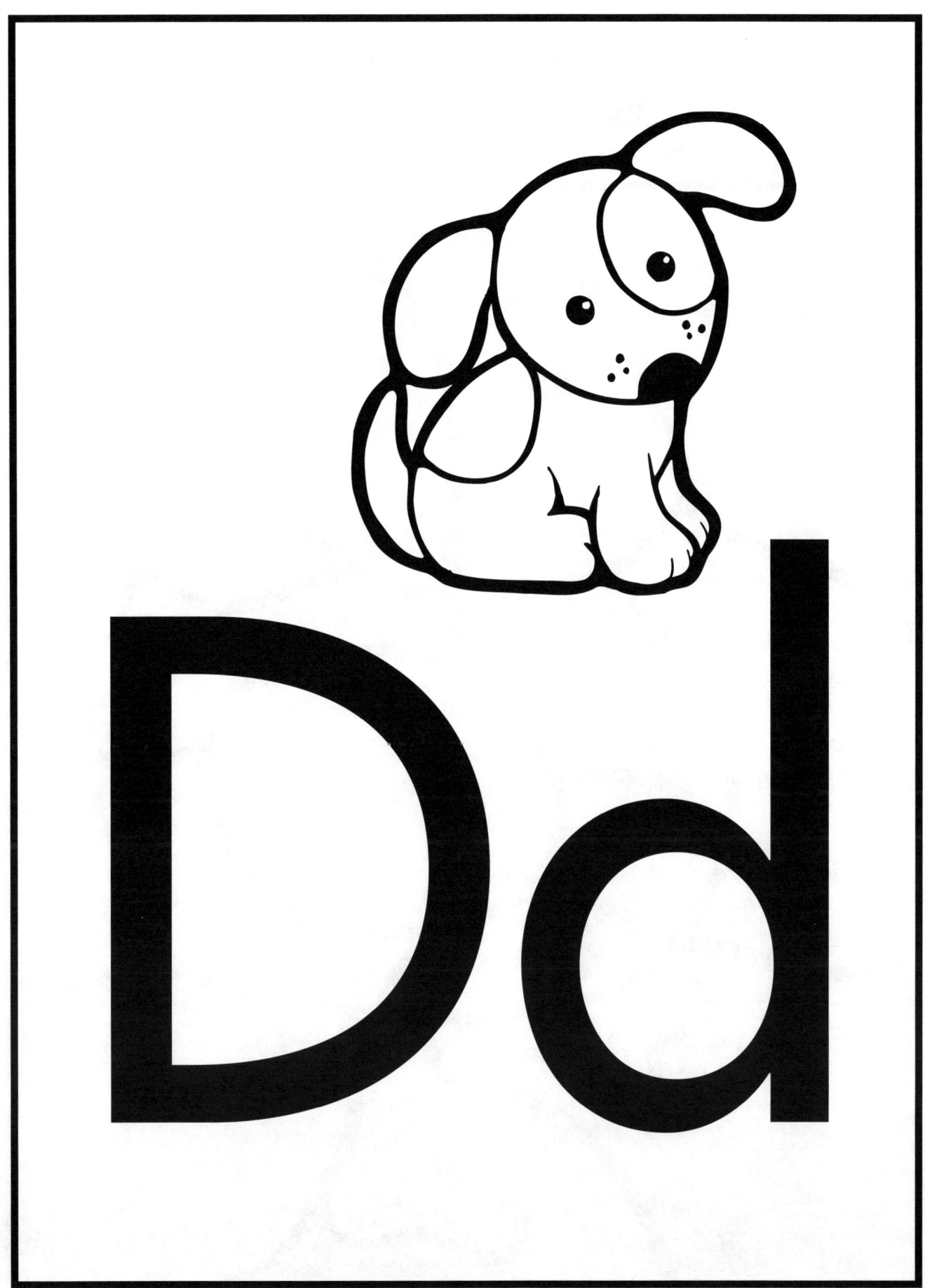

Letter "Dd"

Color the uppercase letters yellow.
Color the lowercase letters orange.

Color the pictures that begin with **D**.

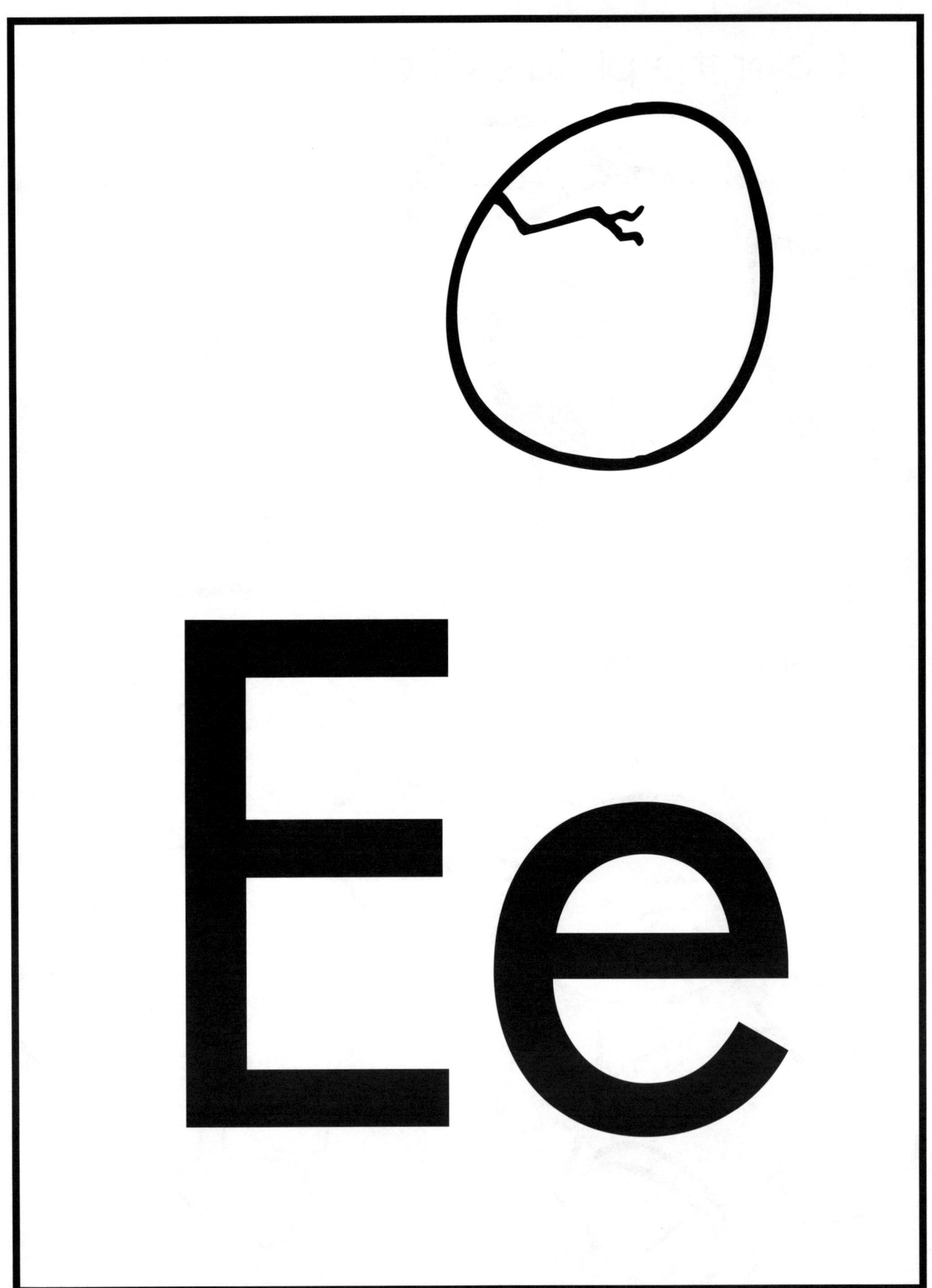

Letter "Ee"
Color the uppercase letters gray.
Color the lowercase letters yellow.

Color the pictures that begin with **E**.

Letter "Ff"

Color the uppercase letters green.
Color the lowercase letters blue.

Color the pictures that begin with **F**.

Letter "Gg"

Color the uppercase letters yellow.
Color the lowercase letters orange.

Color the pictures that begin with **G**.

Letter "Hh"

Color the uppercase letters green.
Color the lowercase letters light blue.

Color the picture that begin with **H**.

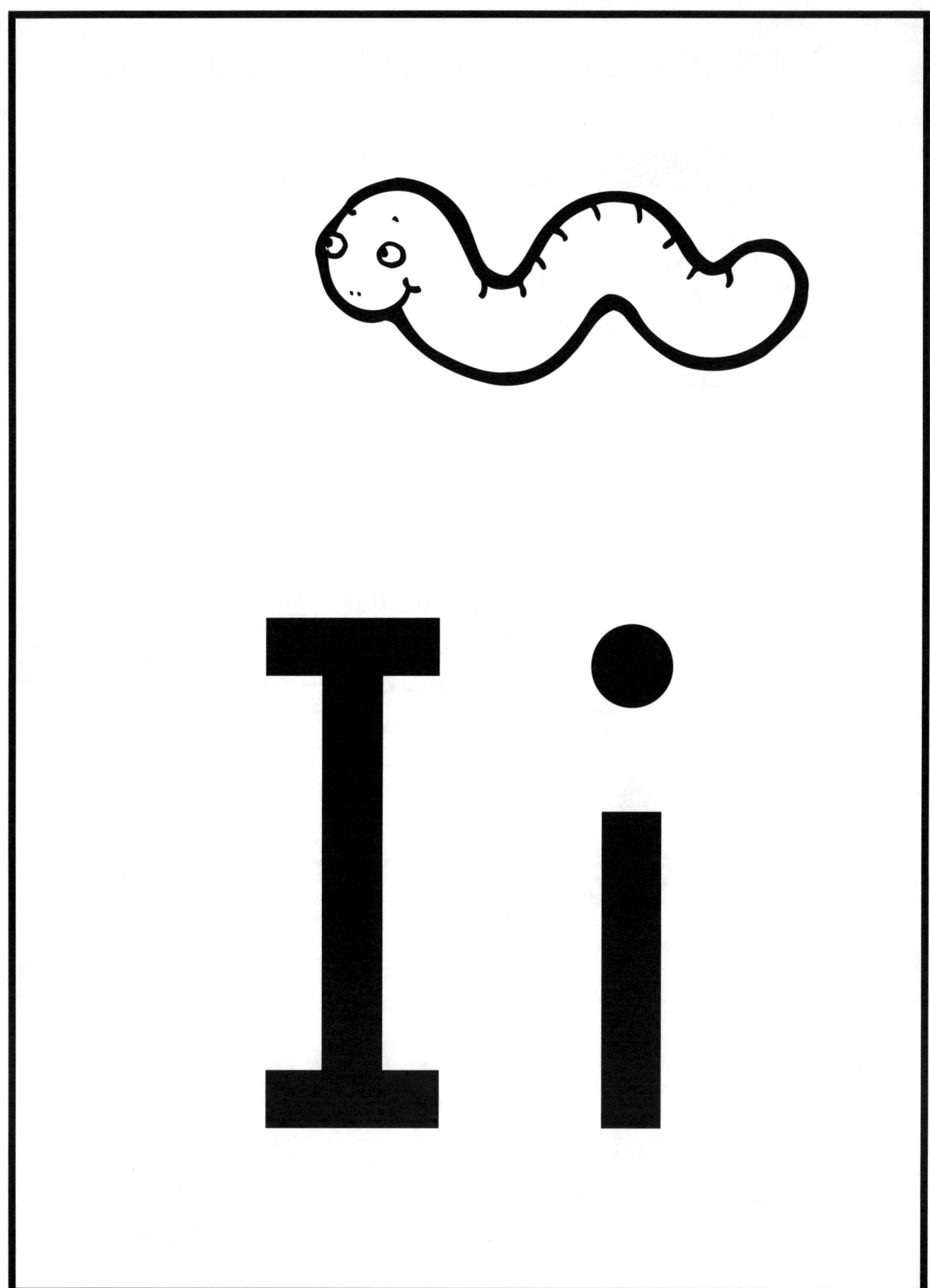

Letter "Ii"

Color the upper case letters brown.
Color the lowercase letters blue.

Color the pictures that begin with I.

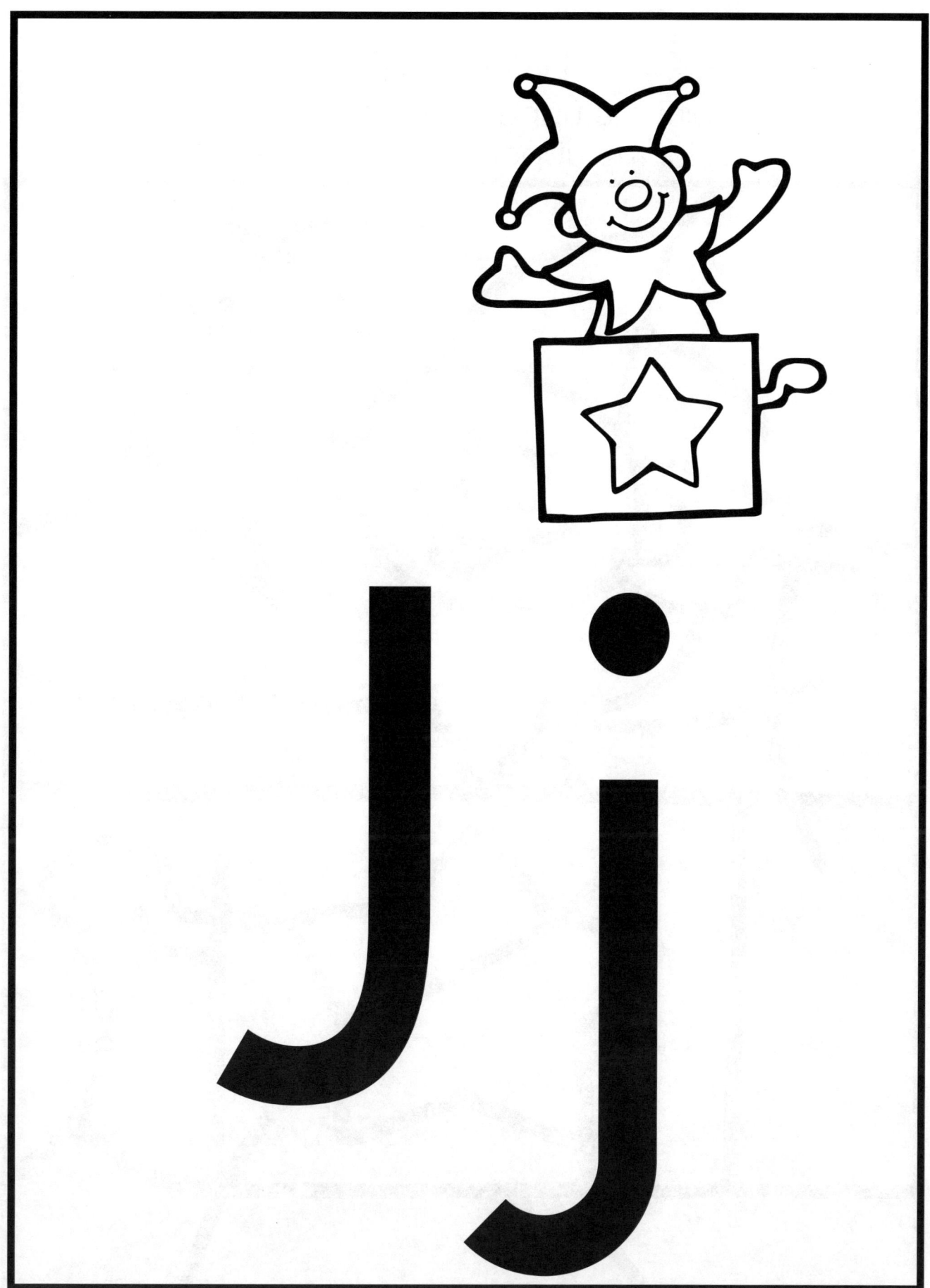

Letter "Jj"
Color the uppercase letters green.
Color the uppercase letters yellow.

Color the pictures that begin with **J**.

Letter "Kk"

Color the uppercase letters red.
Color the lowercase letters gray.

Color the pictures that begin with **K**.

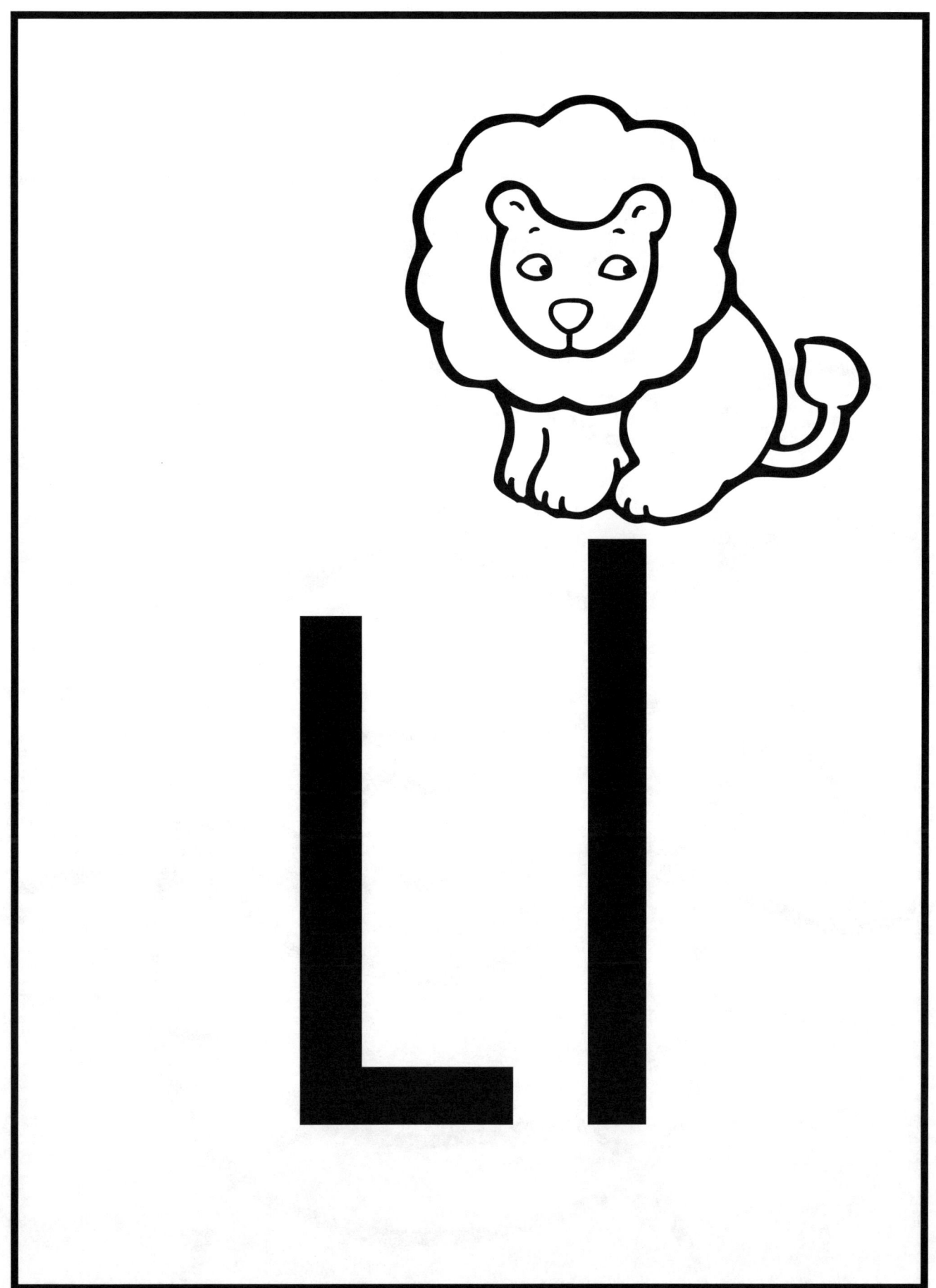

Letter "Ll"

Color the uppercase letters purple.
Color the lowercase letters pink.

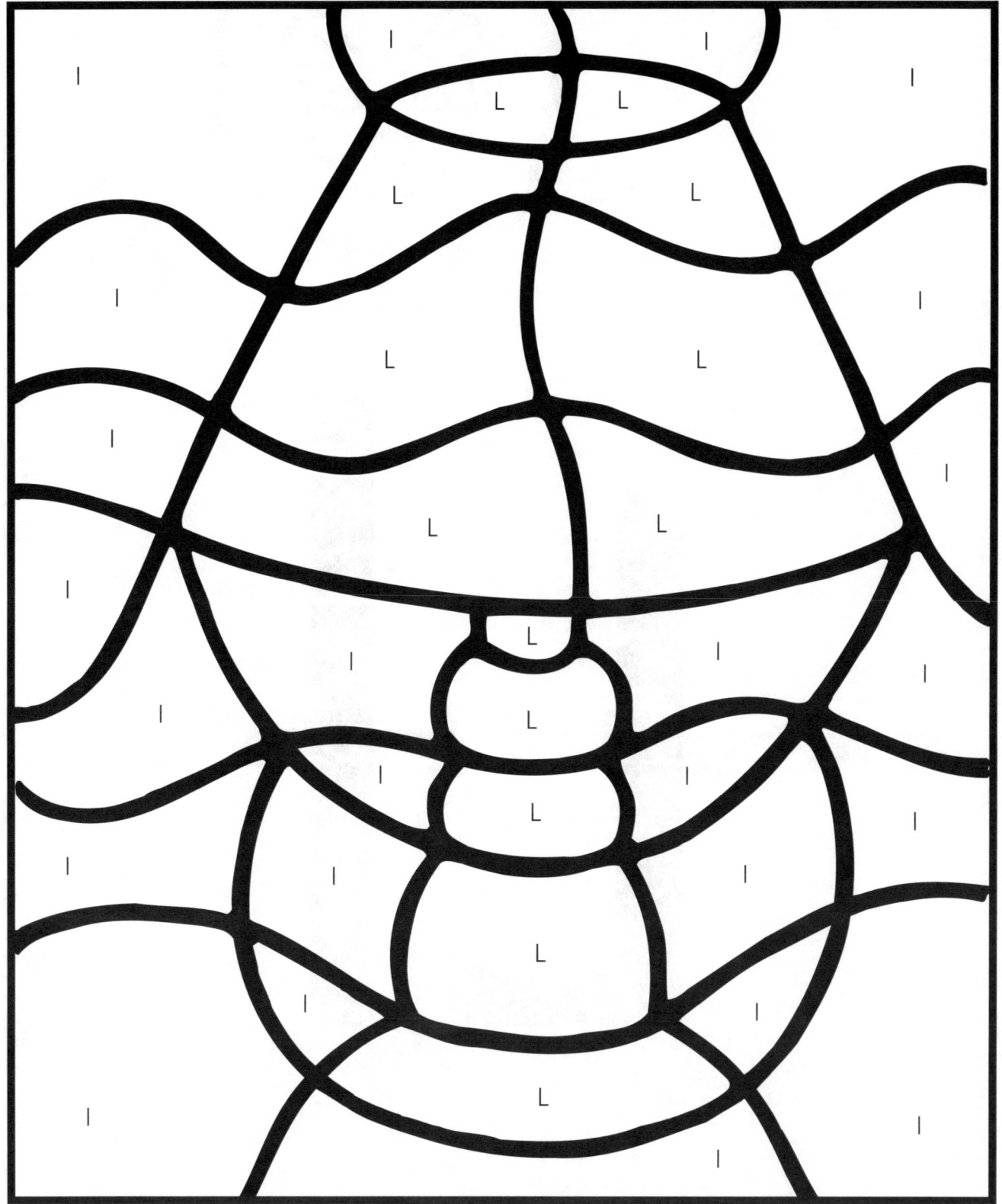

Color the pictures that begin with L.

Letter "Mm"

Color the uppercase letters yellow.
Color the lowercase letters black.

Color the pictures that begin with **M**.

Letter "Nn"

Color the uppercase letters green.
Color the lowercase letters brown.

Color the pictures that begin with **N**.

Letter "Oo"

Color the uppercase letters brown.
Color the lowercase letters blue.

Color the pictures that begin with **O**.

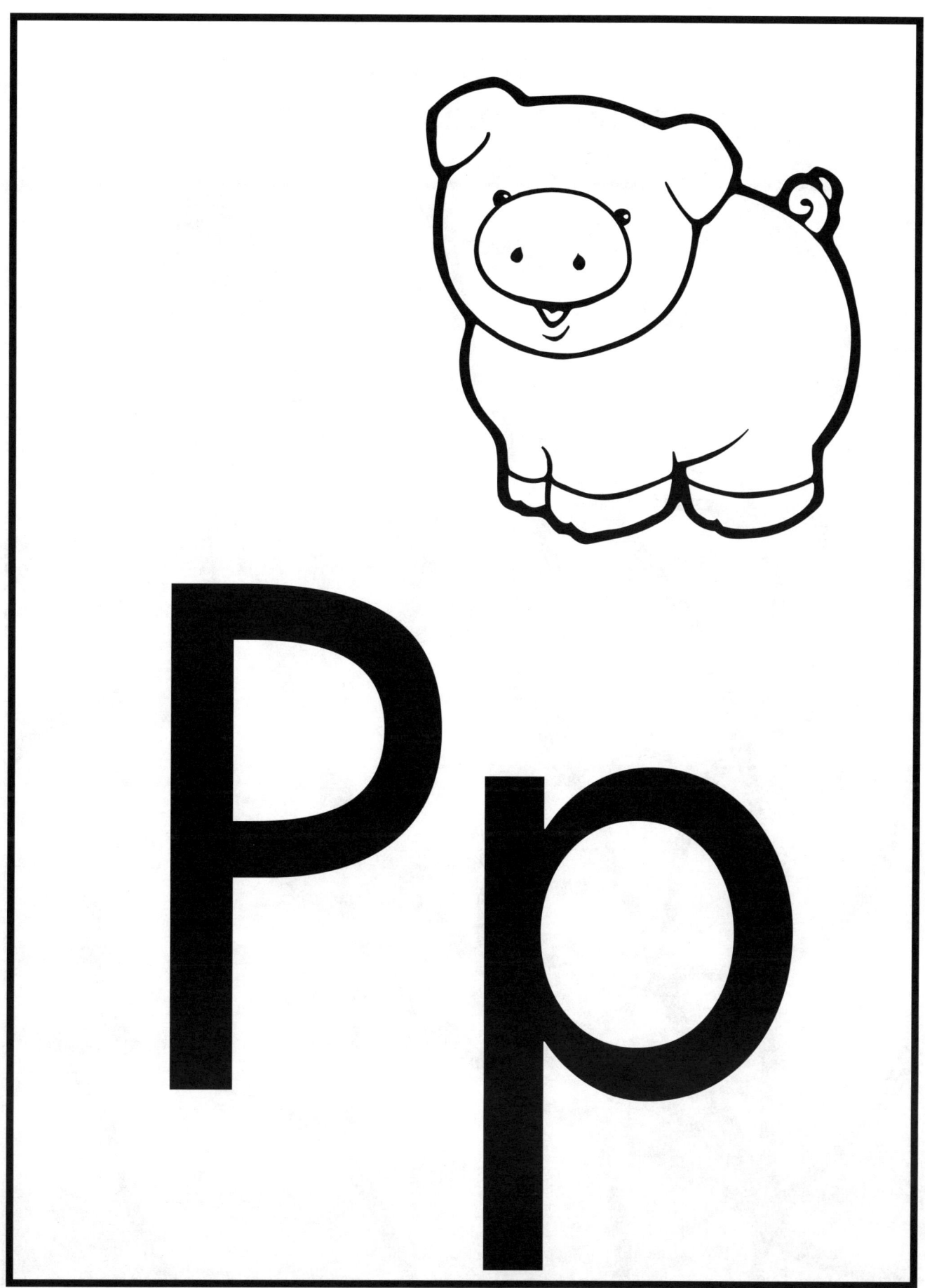

Letter "Pp"

Color the uppercase letters dark green.
Color the lowercase letters light green.

Color the pictures that begin with **P**.

Letter "Qq"

Color the uppercase letters purple.
Color the lowercase letters orange.

Color the pictures that begin with **Q**.

Letter "Rr"

**Color the uppercase letters pink.
Color the lowercase letters green.**

Color the pictures that begin with **R**.

Letter "Ss"

Color the uppercase letters yellow.
Color the lowercase letters green.

Color the pictures that begin with **S**.

Letter "Tt"

Color the uppercase letters green.
Color the lowercase letters blue.

Color the pictures that begin with T.

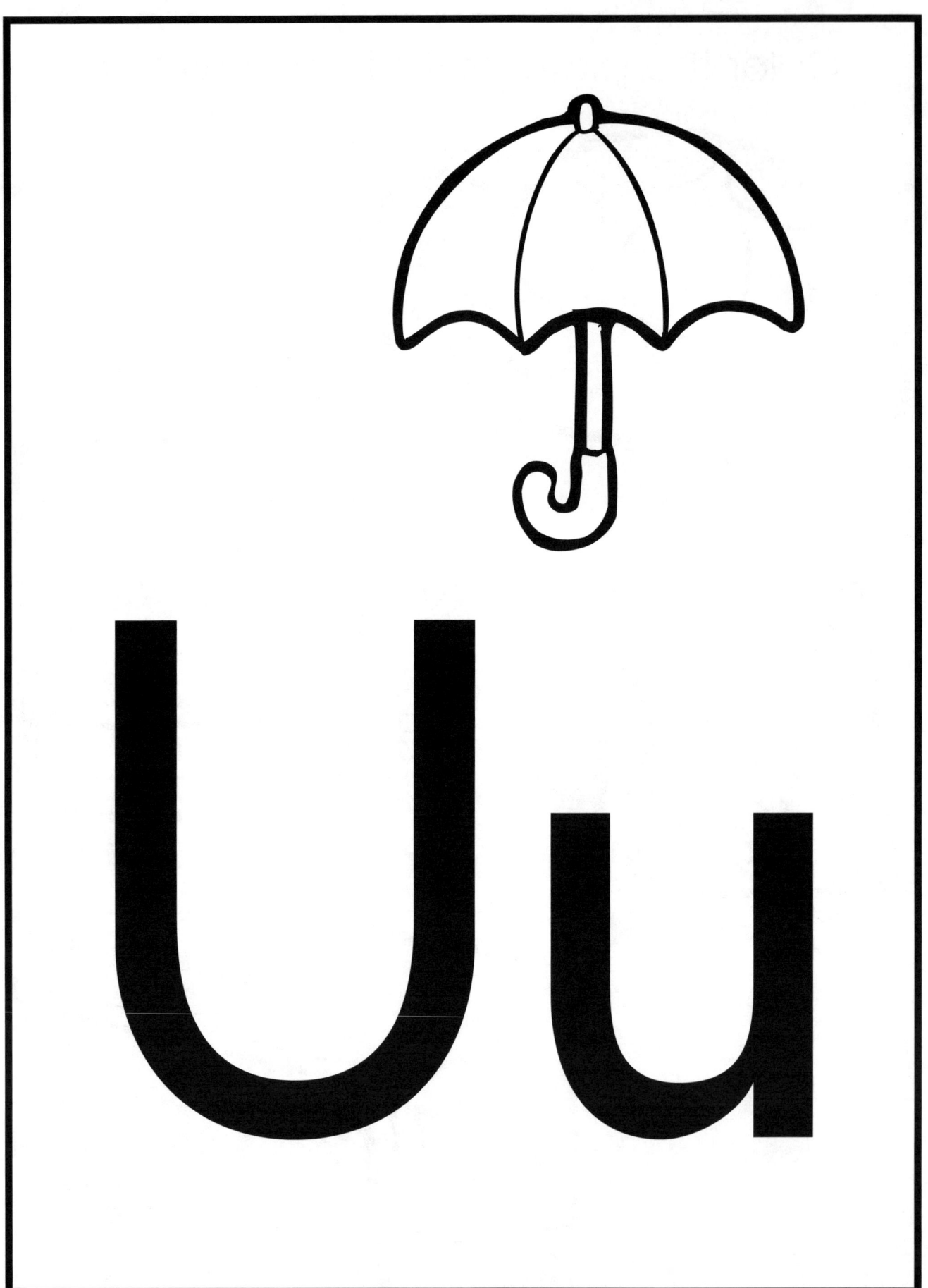

Letter "Uu"
Color the uppercase letters purple
Color the lowercase letters blue.

Color the pictures that begin with **U**.

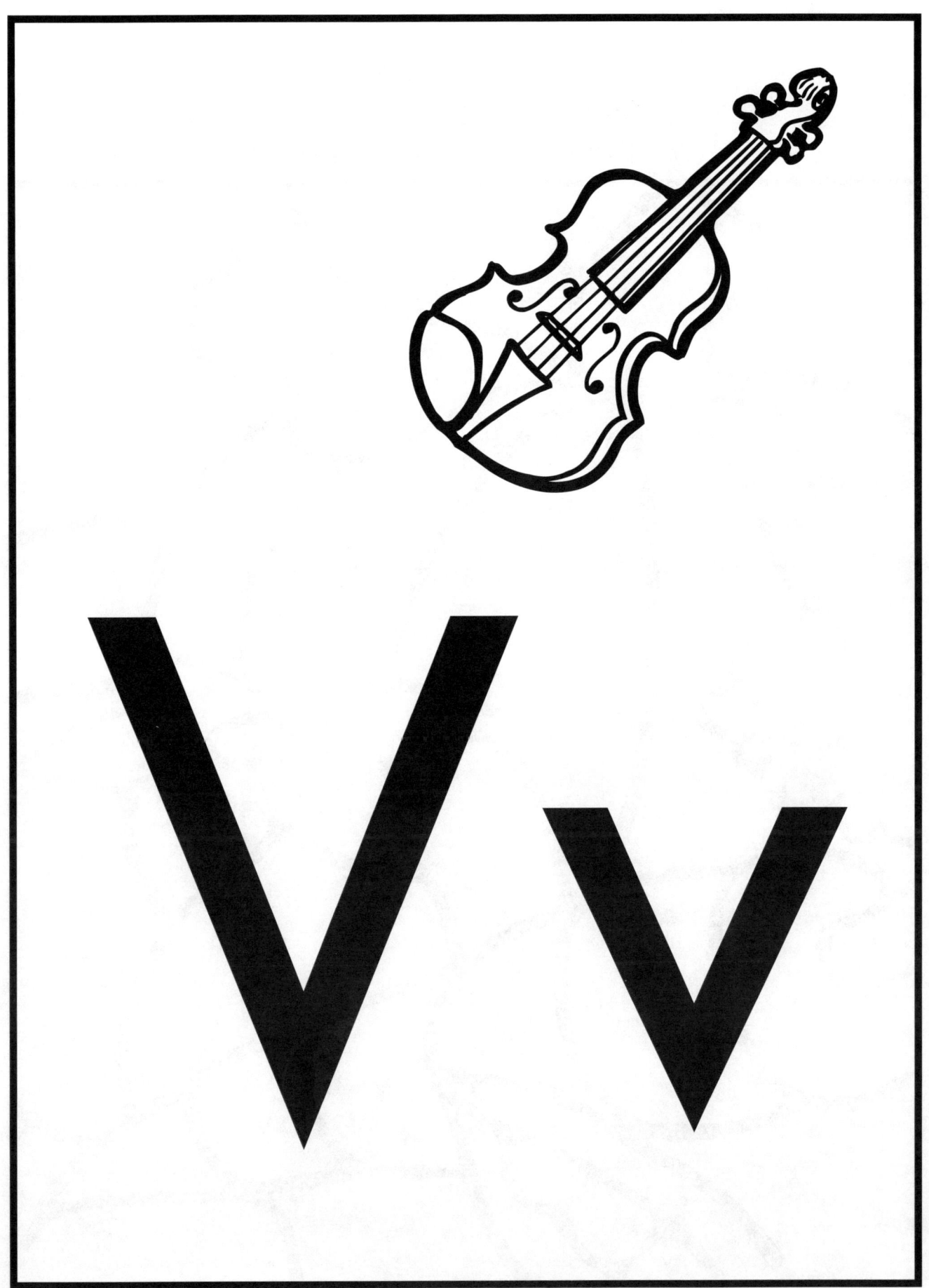

Letter "Vv"

**Color the uppercase letters orange.
Color the lowercase letters green.**

Color the pictures that begin with **V**.

Letter "Ww"

Color the uppercase letters red.
Color the lowercase letters gray.

Color the pictures that begin with **W**.

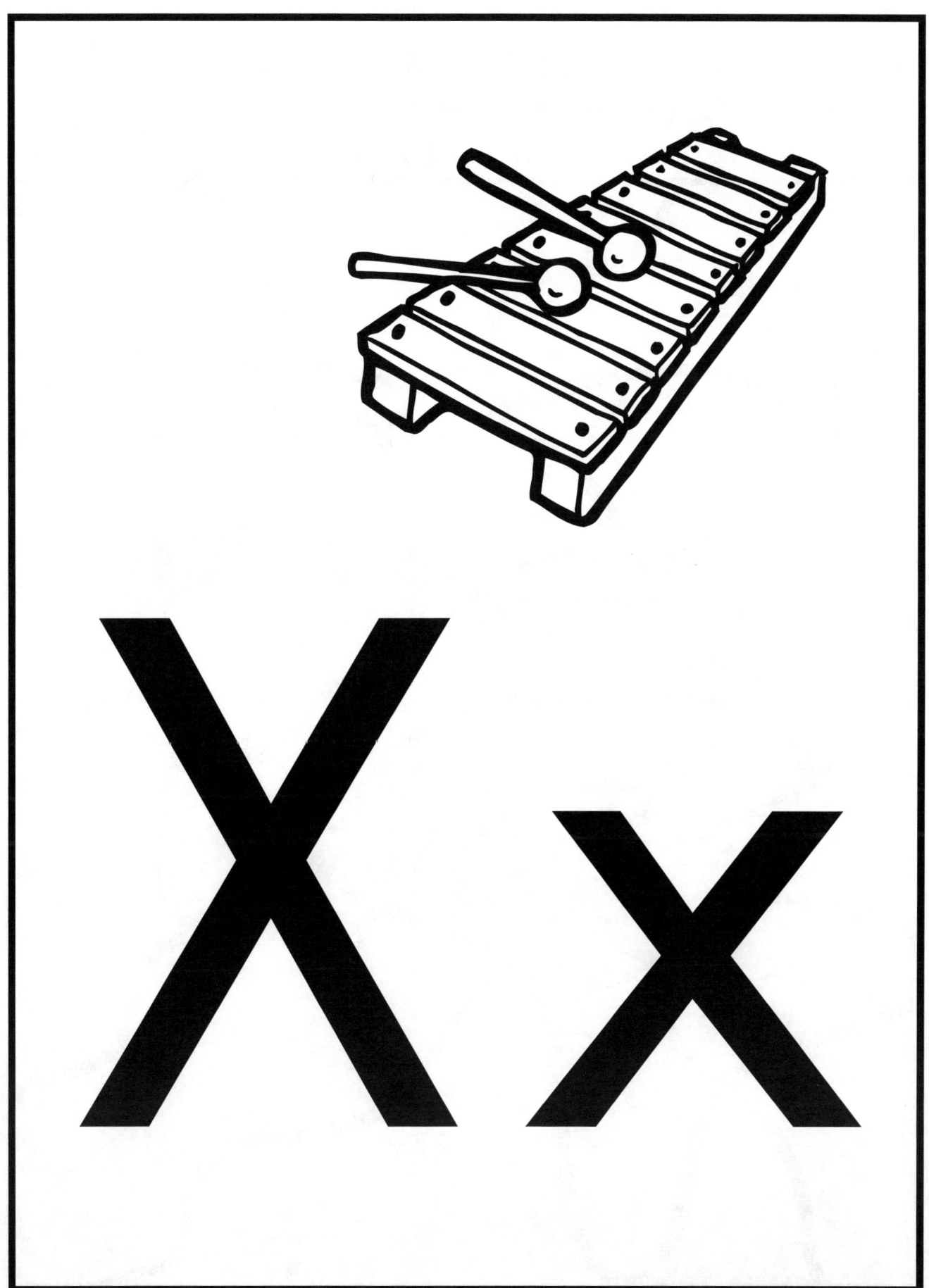

Letter "**Xx**"

Color the uppercase letters gold.
Color the lowercase letters blue.

Color the pictures that begin with **X**.

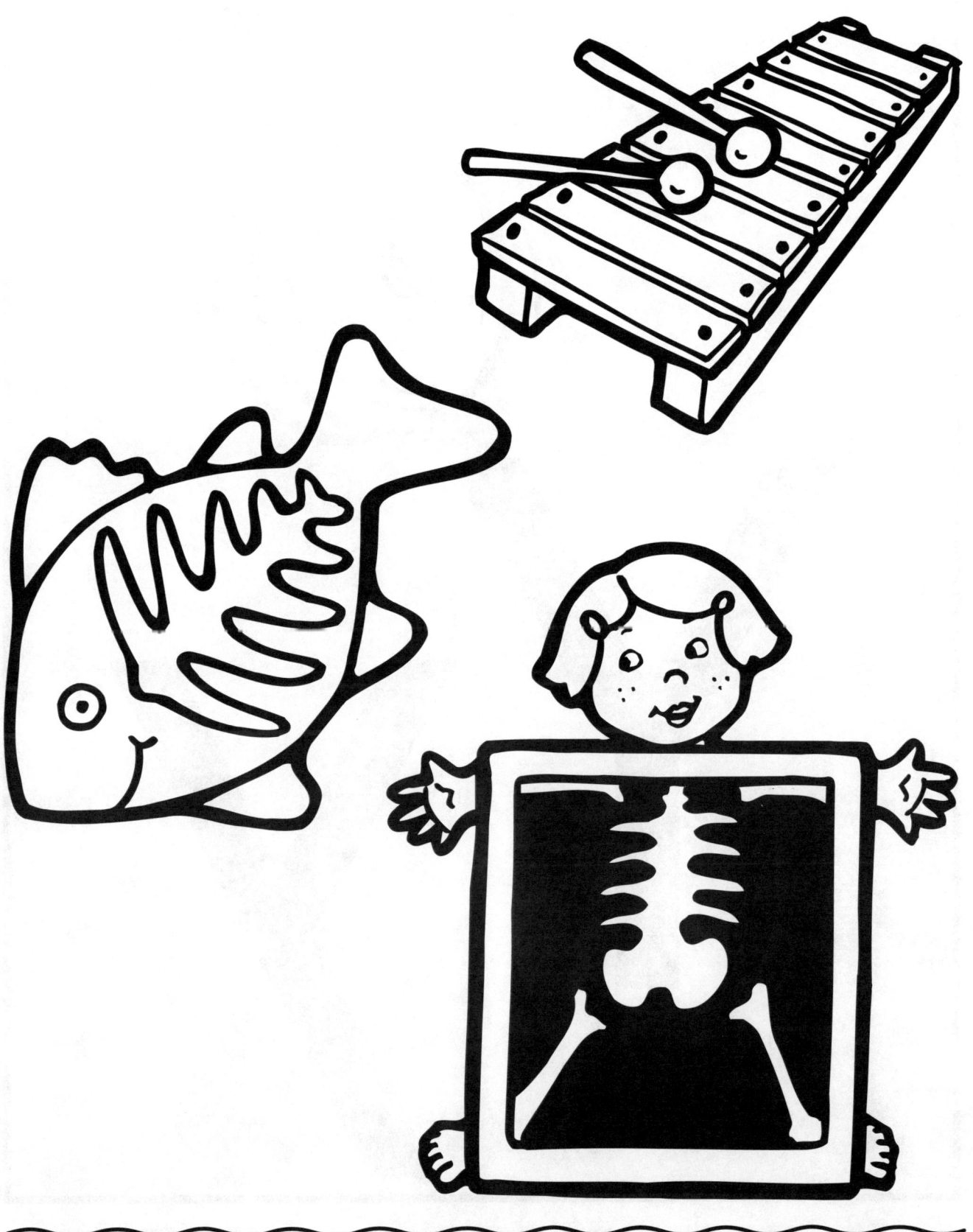

Letter "Yy"

Color the uppercasee letters red.
Color the lowercase letters purple.

Color the pictures that begin with Y.

Letter "Zz"

Color the uppercase letters green.
Color the lowercase letters brown.

Color the pictures that begin with Z.

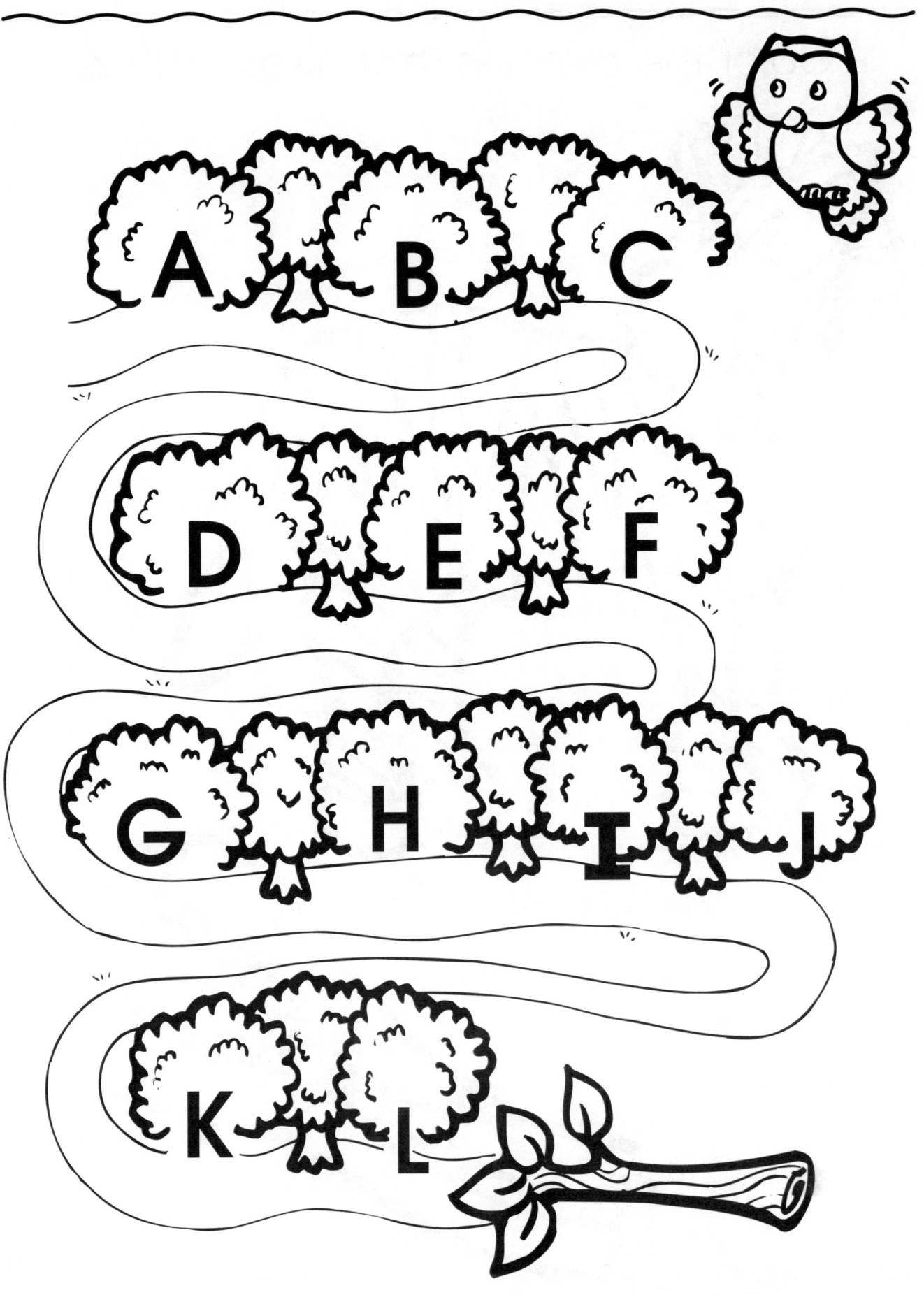

lion

elephant

chimpanzee

giraffe

hippo

parrot

tiger

crocodile

hyena

turtle

guinea pig

hamster

pony

gerbil

rabbit

Birds, Bugs, and Other Creepy Crawlies

  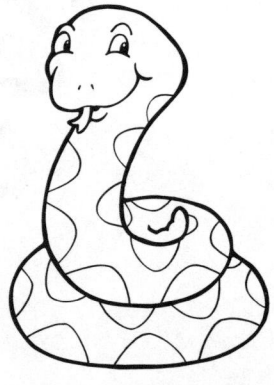

blue jay

robin

woodpecker

bumble bee

ladybug

beetle

spider

fly

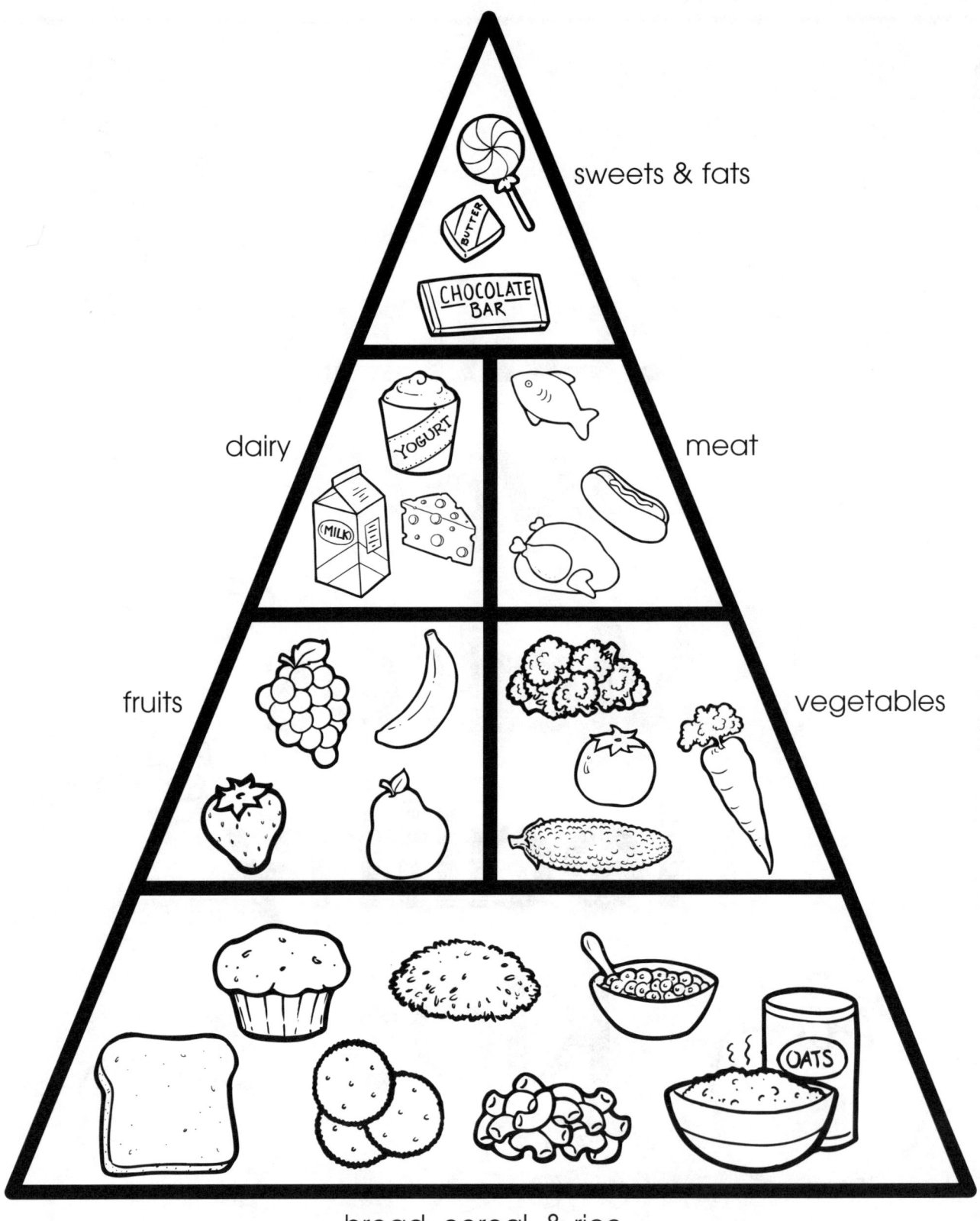

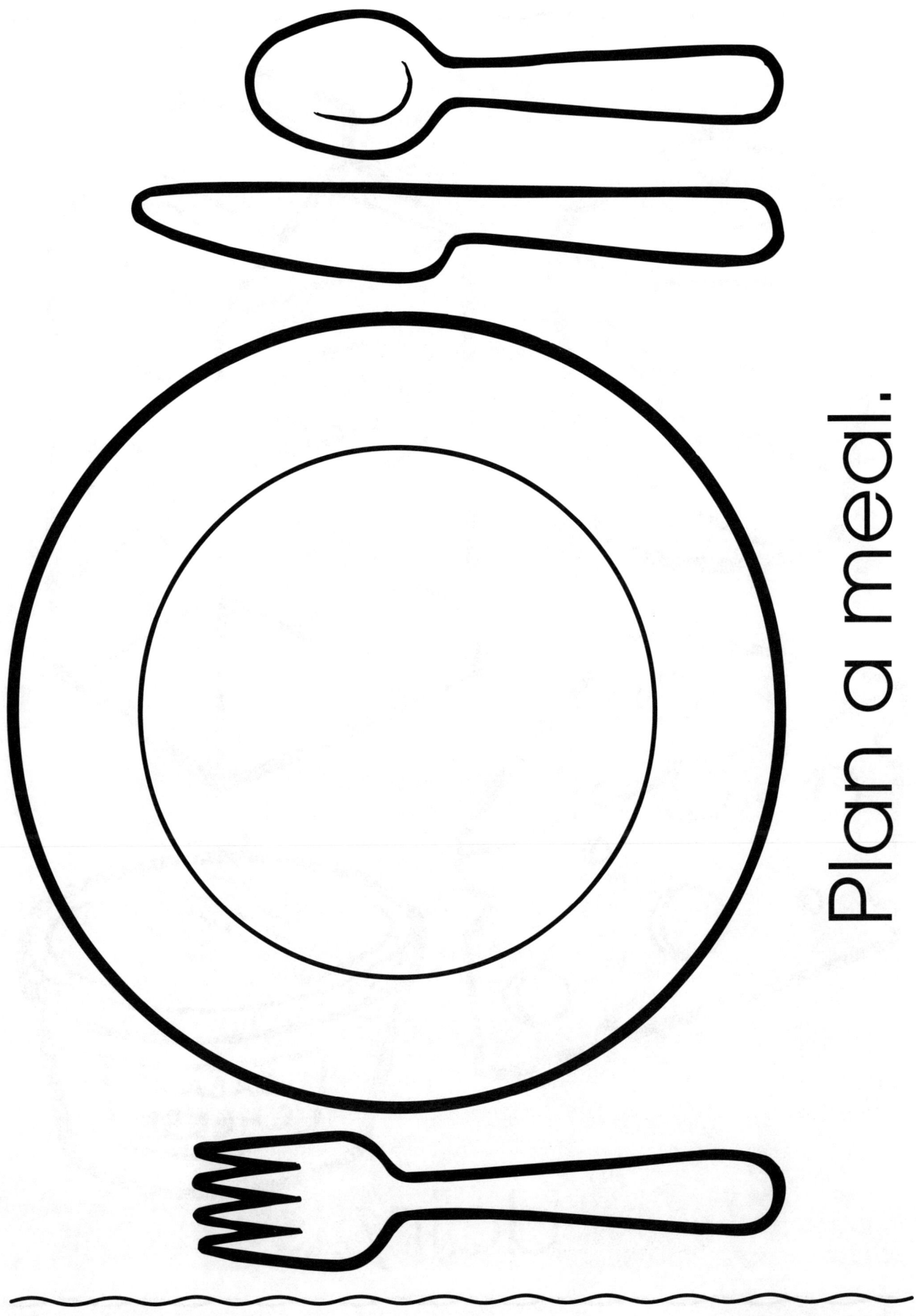

Plan a meal.

dairy

meat and cheese

fruits

vegetables

breads and rice

sweets and fats

Brush your teeth after you eat.

I am a healthy, growing girl.

I am a healthy, growing boy.

Months of the Year

Sunday	Monday	Tuesday	Wednesday	Thursday	Friday	Saturday

Sunday	Monday	Tuesday	Wednesday	Thursday	Friday	Saturday

Sunday	Monday	Tuesday	Wednesday	Thursday	Friday	Saturday

April

Sunday	Monday	Tuesday	Wednesday	Thursday	Friday	Saturday

Sunday	Monday	Tuesday	Wednesday	Thursday	Friday	Saturday

June

Sunday	Monday	Tuesday	Wednesday	Thursday	Friday	Saturday

July

Sunday	Monday	Tuesday	Wednesday	Thursday	Friday	Saturday

Sunday	Monday	Tuesday	Wednesday	Thursday	Friday	Saturday

September

Sunday	Monday	Tuesday	Wednesday	Thursday	Friday	Saturday

October

Sunday	Monday	Tuesday	Wednesday	Thursday	Friday	Saturday

November

Sunday	Monday	Tuesday	Wednesday	Thursday	Friday	Saturday

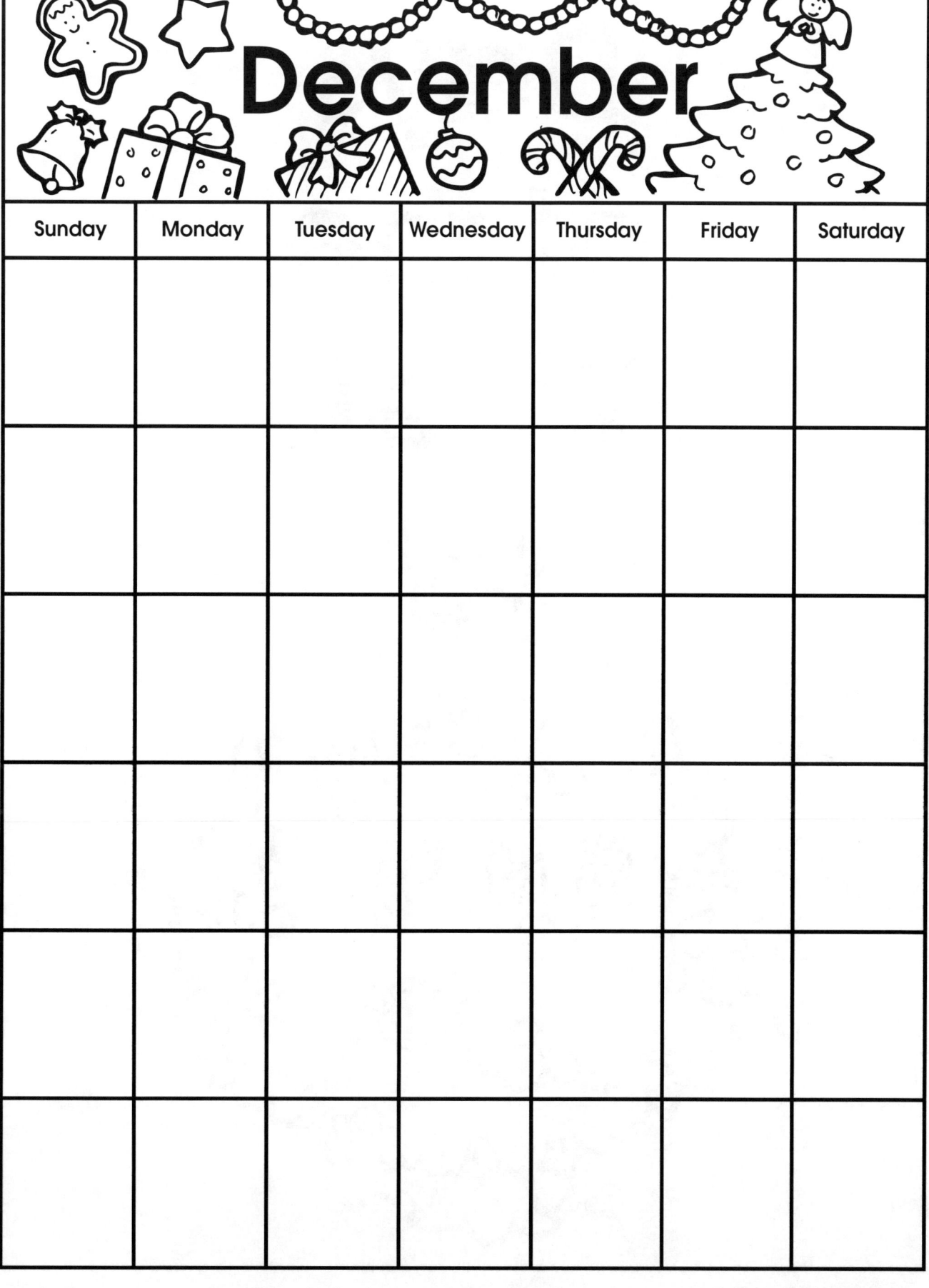

Days of the Week

The Mulberry Bush

Here we go 'round the mulberry bush.
The mulberry bush, the mulberry bush.
Here we go 'round the mulberry bush,
So early in the morning.

Monday

This is the way we wash our clothes,
Wash our clothes, wash our clothes.
This is the way we wash our clothes,
So early Monday morning.

Tuesday

This is the way we iron our clothes,
Iron our clothes, iron our clothes.
This is the way we iron our clothes,
So early Tuesday morning.

Wednesday

This is the way we mend our clothes,
Mend our clothes, mend our clothes.
This is the way we mend our clothes,
So early Wednesday morning.

Thursday

This is the way we sweep our floor,
Sweep our floor, sweep our floor.
This is the way we sweep our floor,
So early Thursday morning.

Friday

This is the way we scrub our floor,
Scrub our floor, scrub our floor.
This is the way we scrub our floor,
So early Friday morning.

Saturday

This is the way we bake our bread,
Bake our bread, bake our bread.
This is the way we bake our bread,
So early Saturday morning.

Sunday

This is the way we go to church,
Go to church, go to church.
This is the way we go to church,
So early Sunday morning.

Seasonal and Holiday

This season is autumn.

Columbus Day

fall leaves

squirrel

owl

apples

scarecrow

cat

turkey

cornucopia

Native American and Pilgrim

birthday cake

dot-to-dot
birthday cake

Santa Claus

ornaments

present

snowperson

stocking

candy cane

wreath

winter scene

Martin Luther King Jr.

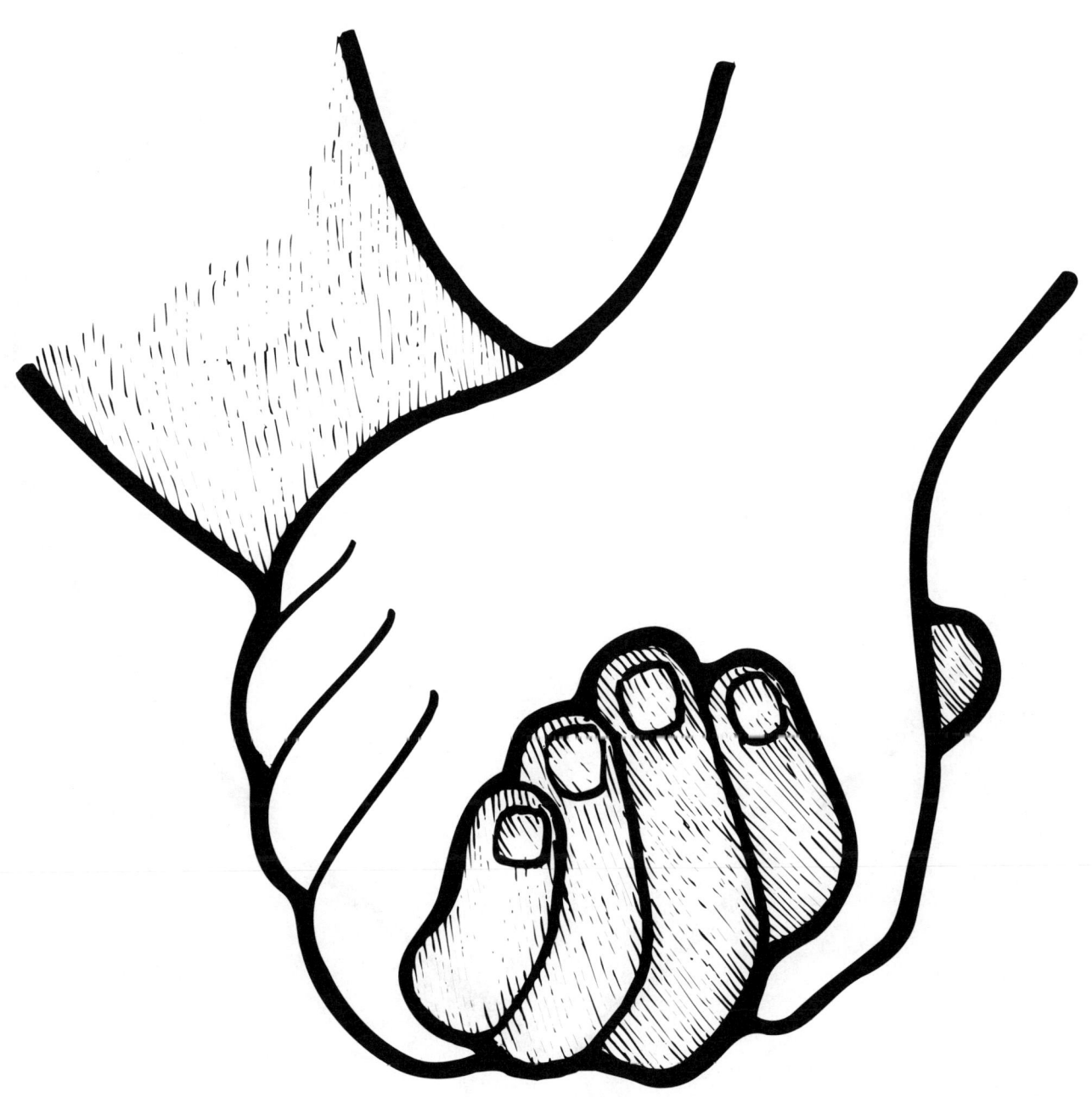

"I have a dream . . ."

heart

valentine

hearts

cupid

Abraham Lincoln

George Washington

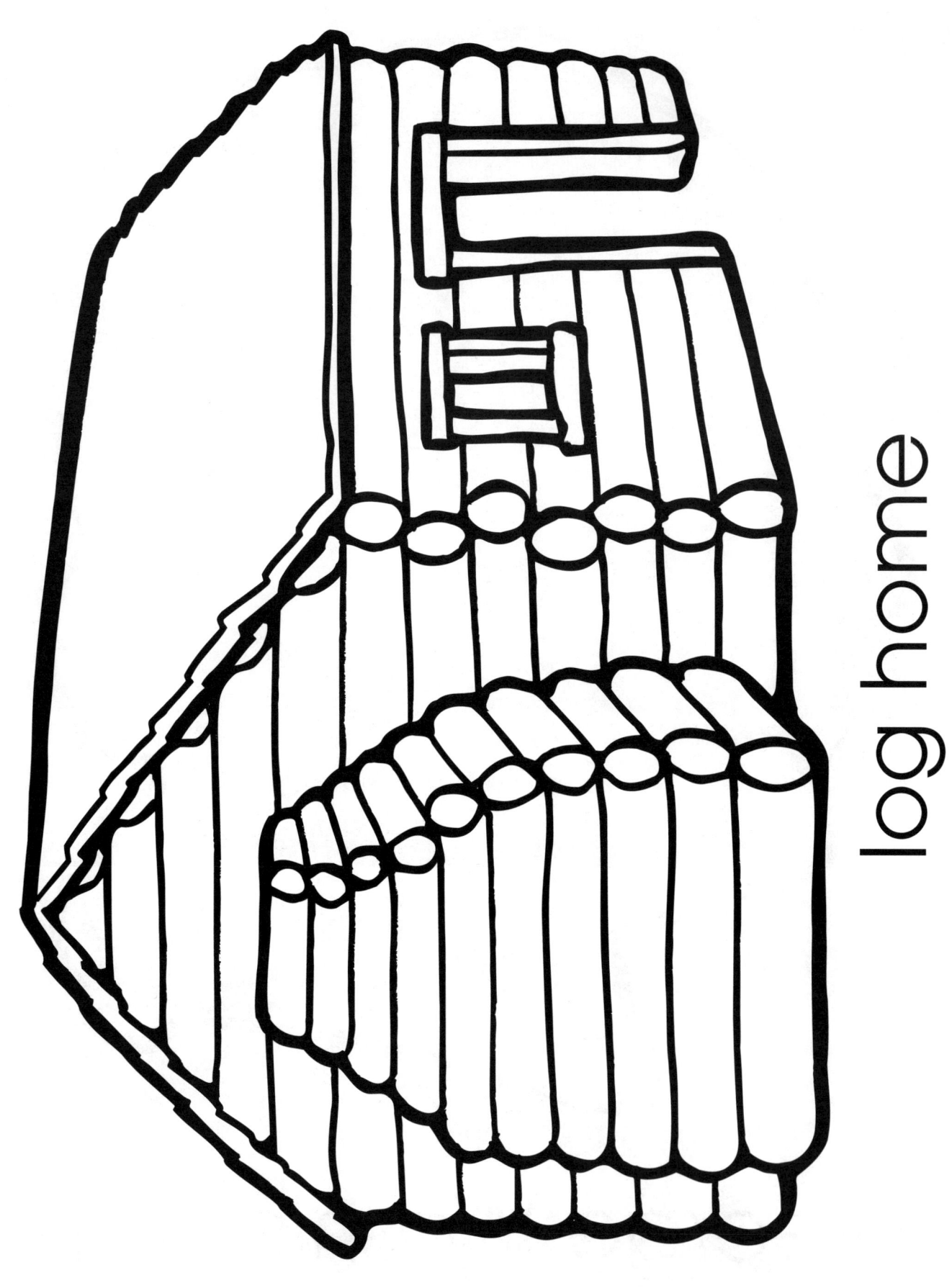

log home

cherry tree

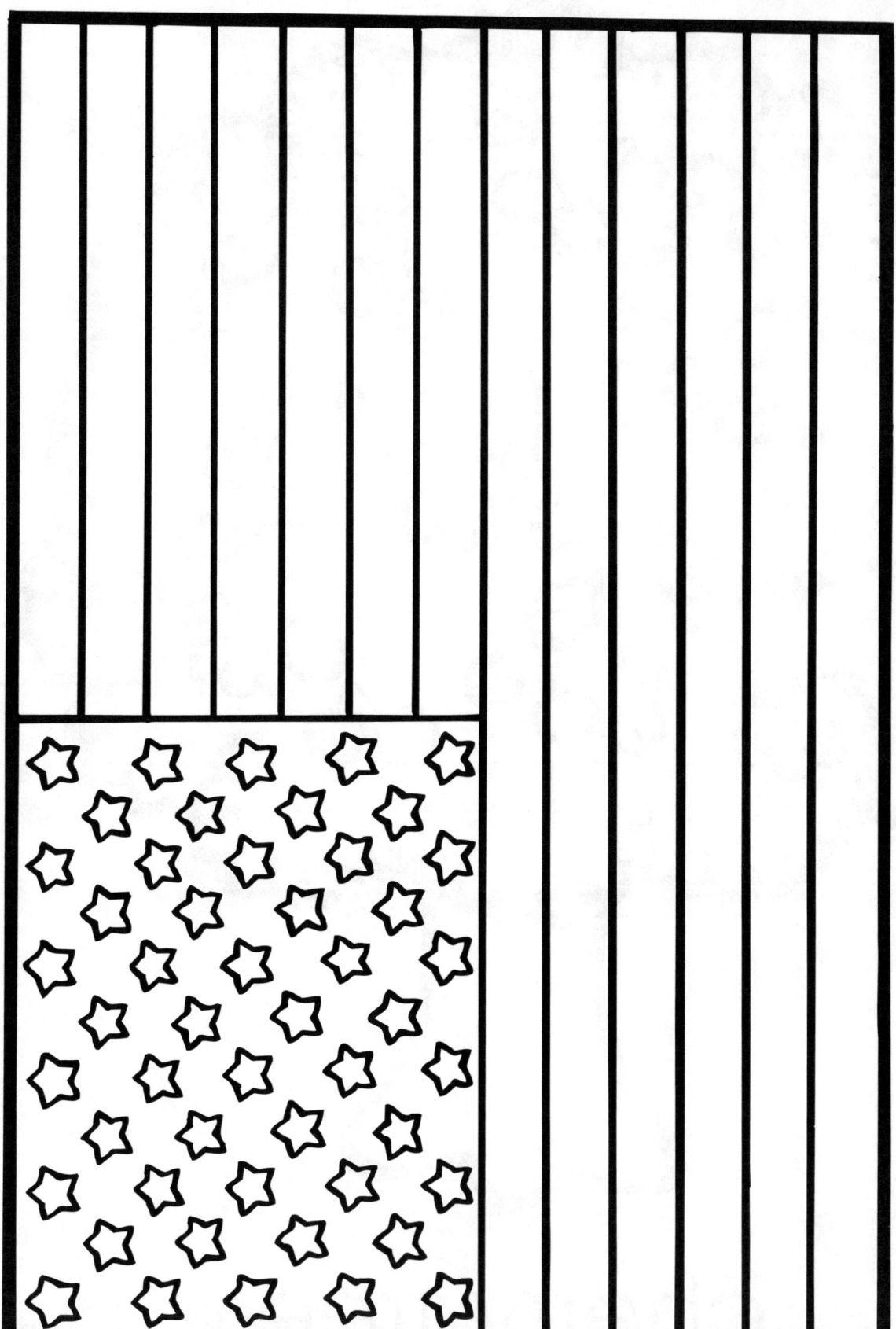

American flag

I pledge allegiance to the flag of the United States of America and to the Republic for which it stands, one Nation under God, indivisible, with liberty and justice for all.

Pledge of Allegiance

shamrock

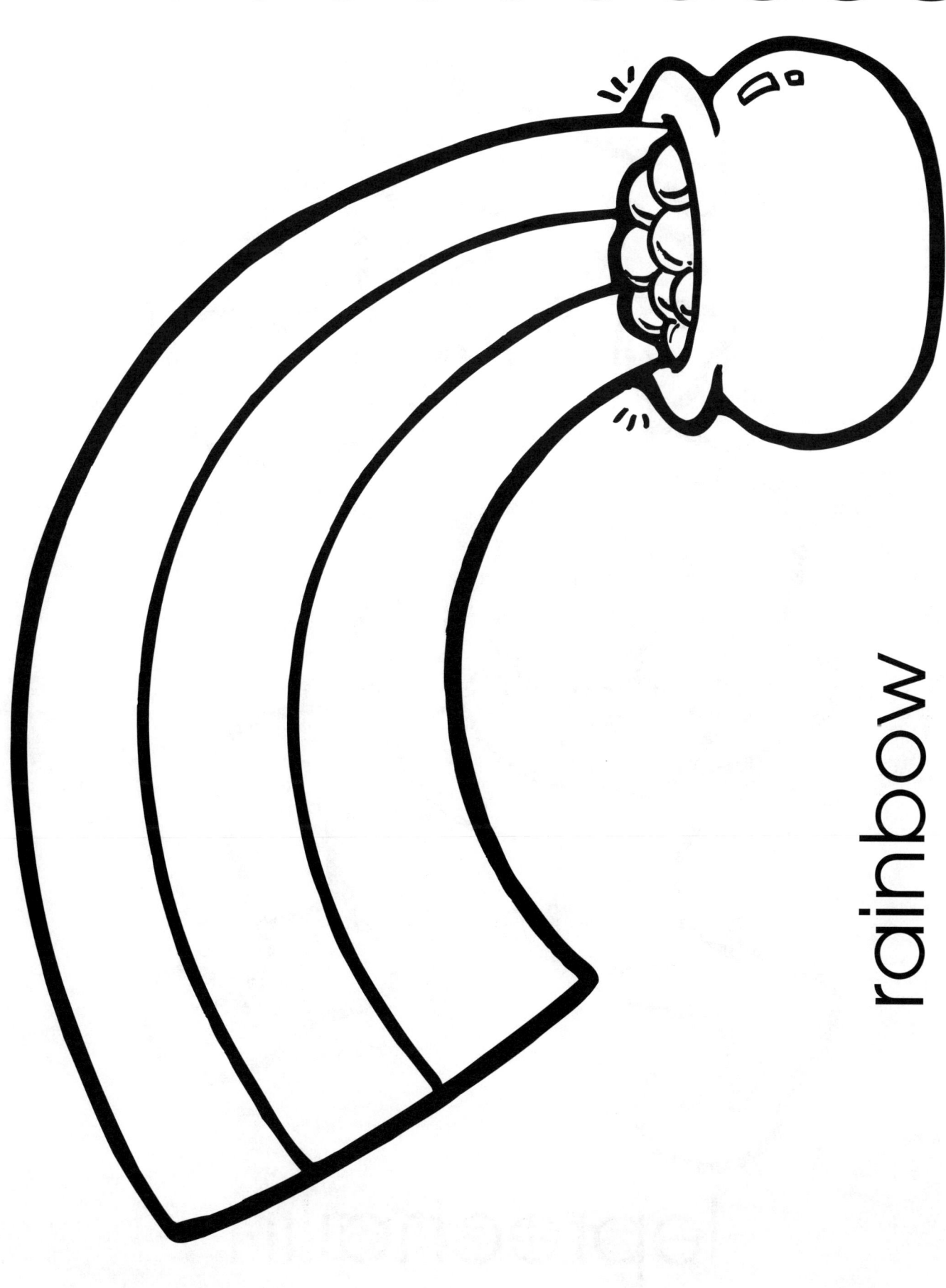

leprechaun

kite

lion and lamb

flowers

chick

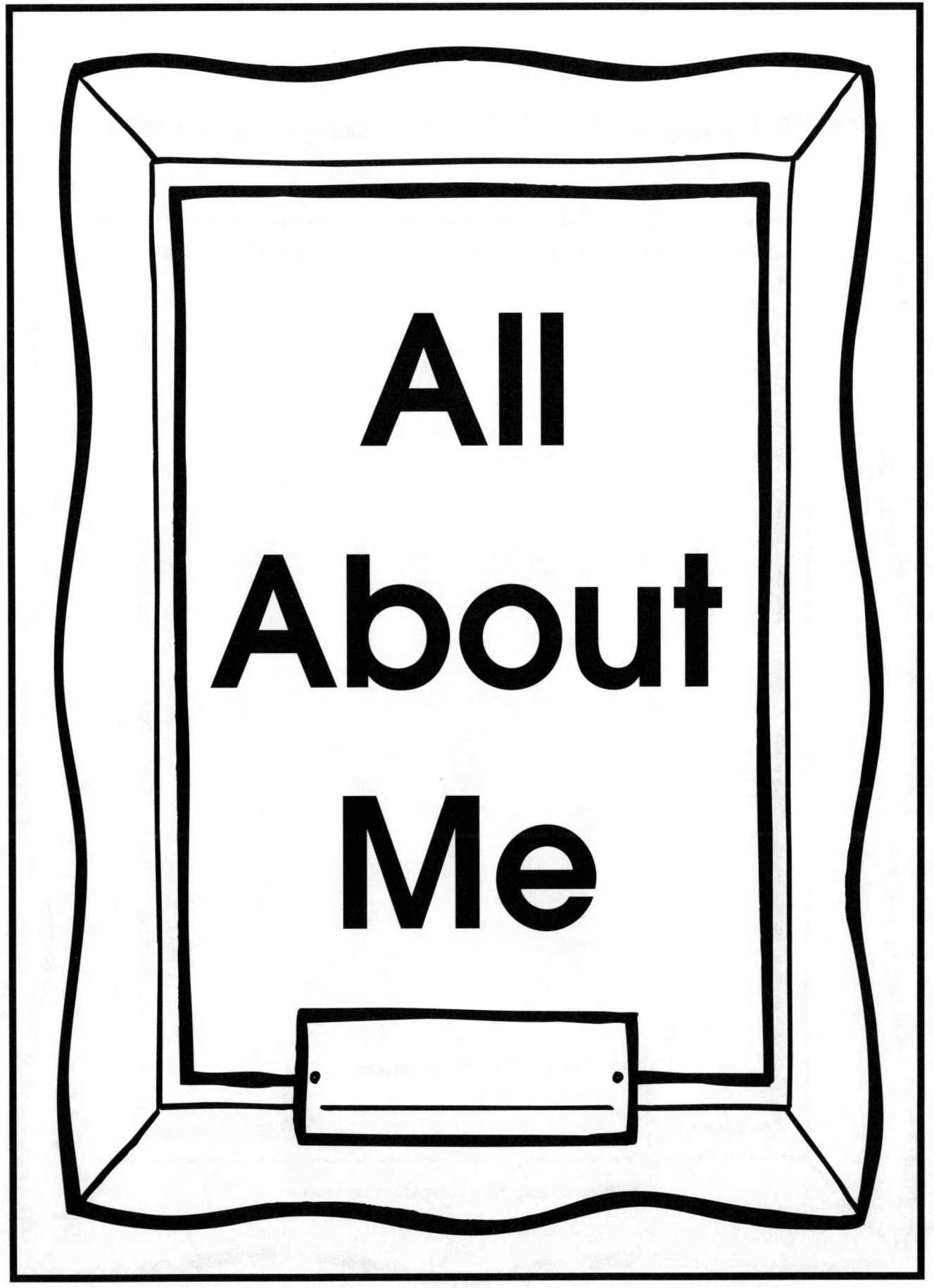

This is a picture of me.

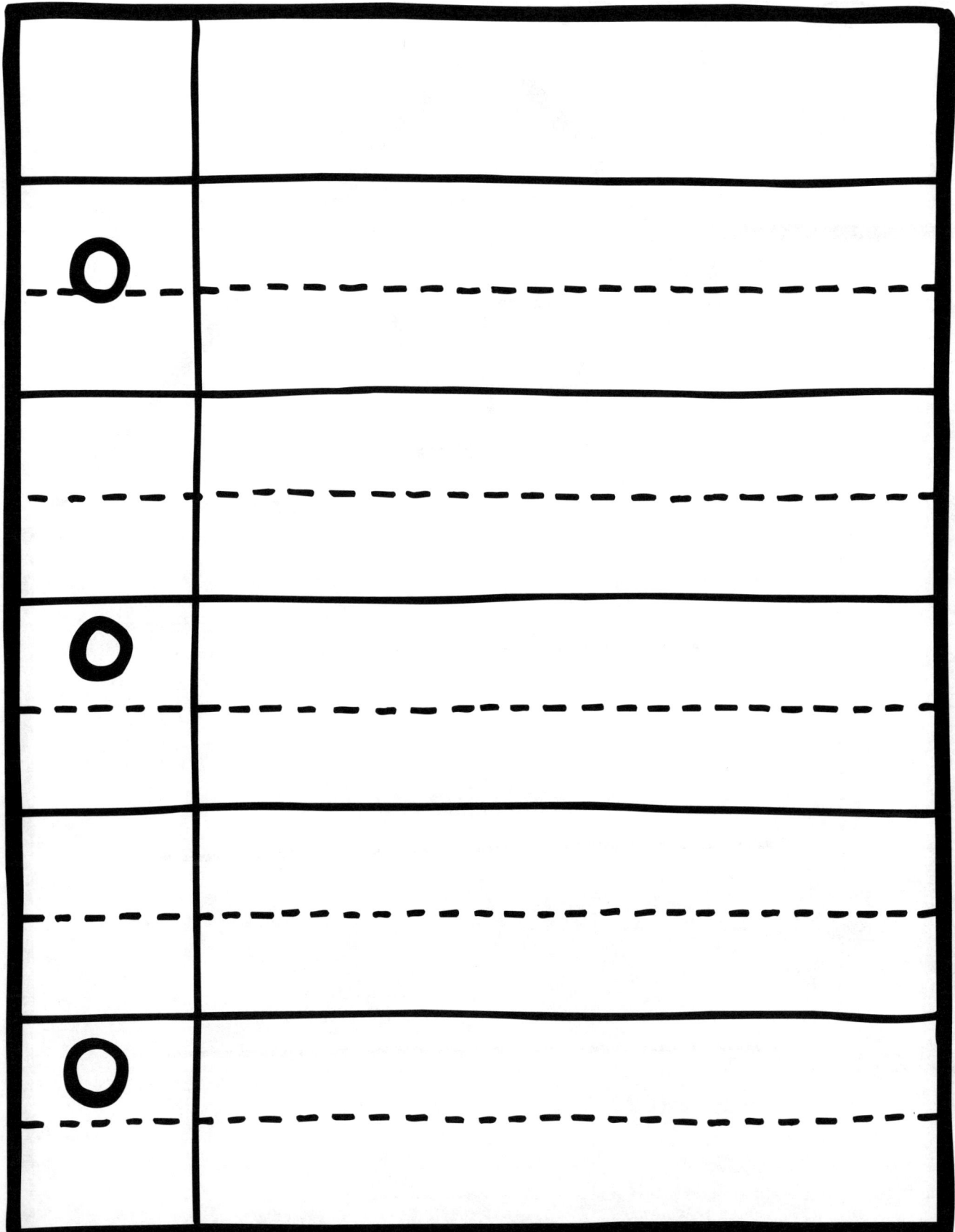

I can print my name.

I know my address.

I know my telephone number.

This is my family.

This is my pet.

This is what I think I will look like when I grow up.

This is my favorite toy.

This is my room.

This is my house.

I am special because . . .

Puzzle Fun

Bunny Maze

Help the lost bunny find its lunch.

Mouse Maze
Help the mouse find the cheese.

Lost Kitten Maze

Help the lost kitten find the little girl.

Yarn Maze
Help the kitten find the ball of yarn.

Chick Maze

Help the lost chick find its way to the nest.

Dog Maze

Help the dog find its puppies.

Bat Maze
Help the lost fruit bat find the fruit tree.

Bear Maze
Help the bear find the honey pot.

Ski Maze

Help the lost skier find her way to the ski chalet.

Kangaroo Maze

Help the baby kangaroo find its mother's pouch.

Clown Maze

Help the clown find the circus tent.